The Organization
of Judicial Power
in the United States

The Organization
of Judicial Power
in the
United States

Carl McGowan

1967 ROSENTHAL LECTURES
Northwestern University School of Law

NORTHWESTERN UNIVERSITY PRESS
Evanston, Illinois

Carl McGowan is a member of the United States Court of Appeals for the District of Columbia Circuit.

Foreword

A LECTURE DELIVERED in an academic environment is in an ancient tradition and has, accordingly, an integrity of its own. I have, accordingly, adhered in what follows to the words as they were spoken at the Northwestern University School of Law on three successive days in December, 1967, although the inevitable delay in reaching print has provided beguiling opportunities for change or addition in the light of intervening events or maturing reflection.

Resistance of these temptations has proved to be less formidable than usual because, in the interval, the litigation avalanche has thundered on. Its growing reverberations have only seemed to me to make more timely and relevant a preoccupation with the organization and functioning of judicial power in both its aspects, federal and state, and with an accommodation of the two which

v

enables each to make its greatest contribution to the fair and efficient administration of justice. The interim period has also seen a quickening of tensions in the academic communities themselves which bring into sharp focus the concept of respect for law. The depth and durability of that respect, and the extent to which we can insist that it be forthcoming, are greatly dependent upon the efficacy of the arrangements by which law is, through the medium of the courts, defined and enforced.

I wish I could be as sure of the usefulness of my observations on this subject as I am of its urgent importance. Doubts on the former score are, however, due only to my own limitations, and not to the three of my law clerks without whose generous and invaluable help the values of timeliness alone could not have been realized. They are Francis M. Gregory, Jr., Michael E. Patterson, and George A. Ranney, Jr.

CARL McGOWAN

Contents

I

The Phenomenon
of Dual Court
Systems

F OR ONE WHO CAME OF AGE in the economic aftermath of 1929 and who, only a few years later, saw the federal powers that were used to disperse depression mobilized on an even larger scale to fight and win a war of world-wide dimensions, strange portents are abroad in the land. The novelty derives not so much from their content as their source—Washington, the federal city itself, the nerve center, the problem-solver. There is nothing new about being told that centralization and consolidation in the creation and exertion of governmental power are signposts on the road to decay, as ancient Rome is said to have discovered too late. This doctrine has emanated steadily throughout the life of the American Republic from such disparate sources as Thomas Jefferson and the

Liberty League. It has tended to rise or fall in the hierarchy of political faiths as the holder viewed the federal establishment complacently from within, or disconsolately from without.

What is new is to hear these admonitions from those who are at or near the centers of federal power. Earlier this year the President himself spoke to the White House Conference of Governors of a sound federal-state relationship—"a new kind of Federalism"[1]—to meet the complexities of our time. He posited as the first essential of such a new relationship that "it must delegate increasingly to the states authority and responsibility for the local treatment of local problems."[2] Two influential White House advisers to both Presidents Kennedy and Johnson have sounded the same note. In his Godkin Lectures at Harvard in 1966, Walter Heller strongly urged the merits—and the inevitability, once Vietnam is behind us—of his plan for the return to the states of a significant share of the federal tax revenues. He harked back to de Tocqueville's observation that, while a central sovereignty may successfully be asserted over a continental nation, central administration is doomed to failure; and he quoted his sometime White House associate, Richard Goodwin, as saying of the nation's problems today that "[we] are not wise enough to solve them from the top, nor are there resources enough to solve them from the bottom."[3]

Whether it proves to be true, as Goodwin has more recently prophesied, that the overriding political issue of the 1970's will be that of decentralization of governmental authority,[4] there is currently a striking change of mood—striking because it has occurred in those now wielding great agglomerates of centralized power and who, therefore, are not fairly chargeable with the jaundice of the politically disappointed or dispossessed. In the New Deal and World War II days, and for a long time thereafter, it was not popular in Washington circles to speculate out loud as to whether the laying on of federal hands was the only possible mode of absolution of worldly ills.

I have some personal recollections of this peril because, in the early 1950's, I was in the service of a state government, and became at least mildly enthusiastic about its present and potential capacities to serve well in many areas of human affairs. When, on my infrequent visits to Washington, I would timidly venture these thoughts, my federal fellow bureaucrats to a man regarded me as a soul lost in the outer darkness, one of whom it could most charitably be said that he had gone native under the tedium and debasement of pursuing public employment in a provincial capital. For them, all roads led to Washington, and no social problem of any consequence would yield but to the ministrations of federal authority. Nor, despite their already busy lives, were they ever averse to taking one more burden upon their shoulders.

It is true that their talents matched their assurance—so much so as largely to overshadow their state and local government counterparts. But the balance may be shifting as the greater challenges and opportunities for effective action appear at the grass roots, and as influential voices call attention to this fact. In his address at the Harvard Law School Sesquicentennial Celebration last September, Justice Brennan pointed the way for young lawyers in these words:

> It seems to me that for too long the focus has been almost exclusively on the Federal Government at the expense of state and municipal and other governmental bodies. The flow of talented young lawyers to Washington that began in the 1930's, and that has continued apace through the present time, has yet to be matched by a comparable attraction to state capitals, county and regional government offices, and the like. Yet, our country's problems have clearly changed in nature, and it now is apparent that many of them must be solved at the local and state levels if they are to be solved at all.[5]

It is different today. The mood is one of humility in the shadow of problems assertedly too big for any one government, even though it be the Goliath centered in

Washington. Harassed mayors and governors are no longer lectured for failing to seek federal help, but are instead sternly reminded that Washington does not have all the answers. It would appear that the normally self-confident federal officeholders have become shatteringly aware of the magnitude of some of the problems that press for action: pollution of the air and water, mass transportation, education, mental health, race relations, housing, crime—so many of which flow from the great migrations of our people to the cities, and which no reasonable man can view without acute feelings of trepidation about the shape of things to come. Even if the nature of the solutions was clear, there remain enormous doubts as to the adequacy of the administrative resources available solely at the federal level. As the President said to the governors in the remarks mentioned earlier:

> Our problem is not political federalism. It is administrative federalism—a system and method whereby the many units of government at the working level coordinate and join their resources to get a job done well.[6]

A cautious and chastened mood in the federal establishment with respect to the limits of its effectiveness will undoubtedly contribute to a revival of interest in strong state and local government.[7] This feeling happens to coincide with the sweeping away—by federal judicial authority, be it duly noted—of one of the great road-blocks to the renovation of local government, i.e., the malapportionment of voting authority between city and country, and the consequent sterilization of the former in its time of greatest need.[8] It also seems likely that there may be in the reasonably near future some redressing of the financial balance between the nation on the one hand and the states on the other. The federal revenues are so substantial that even a small return to the states in percentage terms would involve a significant number of dollars. If the Heller Plan, or anything like it, is ever put into effect, a major realignment of the functional relationships between the federal and the local governments will inevitably accompany it.[9]

The mood, and the prospect it foreshadows, are at least real enough to make it timely to inquire into their significance for that area of governmental power known as the judicial. Would any ponderable alteration in the balance between federal and state authority extend to the respective courts existing under each? Are there difficulties being encountered under the present dual systems which argue for such an extension? Whether or not there be a renascence of local government generally vis-à-vis the national government, what are the forms of accommodation between federal and state judicial power likely to be as the courts grapple with the urgencies of modern life, and will those forms preserve for the federal government its currently commanding position? These are, admittedly, things now to be seen but dimly. But their relevance to the quality of the administration of justice in a generation facing immense challenges warrants their present exploration.

Inferior Federal Courts

Every schoolboy learns by rote at an early age that our system of government is founded upon the principle of the separation of powers into legislative, executive, and judicial. But complications arise when it is remembered that "our" system of government is really two systems—state and national—and that each has been constituted by reference to the same principle of tripartite division. This means that there are two judicial powers —the one that resides in the constitution of each state, and the other that is embedded in Article III of the federal Constitution.[10] It is, of course, inconceivable that any independent and residual sovereignty like an American state should be without a judicial power, but if you were to ask why it was necessary for a state-created government of limited powers like the federal to have one also, you would be raising a question which was repeatedly asked when the new Constitution of the United States was submitted for ratification.

After all, the Articles of Confederation under which the people had lived for several years contained no such power. Despite the fact that it was dissatisfaction with the weak and ineffective nature of those Articles which instigated the Philadelphia Convention, and although there is no evidence that any of the actual participants in that body doubted the desirability of the inclusion of a judicial power, these questions during the ratification period were sufficiently frequent to make Alexander Hamilton take note of them in his pleas for acceptance of the Convention's handiwork.

With the advantage of hindsight, it is possible to accuse Hamilton of either lack of vision or artful dissimulation of the degree to which a national judicial power might touch upon the lives of the citizens. In Federalist No. 78, he invoked the authority of Montesquieu himself by quoting the observation that "of the three powers [that is to say, the legislative, executive, and judicial] . . . the *Judiciary* is next to nothing." And it was in this context that Hamilton gave his famous reassurance that, for the citizen concerned about the impact of government upon himself, the "least dangerous" branch of that government was the judiciary. Assuming, he wrote, a truly independent judiciary, "the general liberty of the citizen can never be endangered from that quarter." [11]

Although it is not the fashion today to take such a *de minimis* view of the potential impact of the judicial power upon the body politic, there were many good reasons, dutifully rehearsed elsewhere by Hamilton,[12] why it was unthinkable that the framers at Philadelphia would have crippled their new government by failing to entrust it with a judicial power. What did divide the Convention was the method by which that power was to be organized. Since judicial power must have its effectuation through a court, it was clear that there must be at least one national court, i.e., the United States Supreme Court. But need there be more, in view of the fact that each state had its own system of trial and appellate tribunals? Could not any claim of federal right be asserted in state court litigation, with its ultimate vindication assured by appeal to the federal Supreme Court, if that should prove necessary?

Although the origins and development of the inferior federal courts pre-empt a wide assortment of legal literature,[13] one may still have the feeling that the significance of their existence has somehow fallen short of adequate recognition. That significance, in my submission, is that the fact of their being has been an imperative in the shaping of a body of law commensurate with the ideals and capacities of a growing and changing nation of continental dimensions. Without the judicial machinery at hand in the form of the lower federal courts, it seems most unlikely that the "one supreme Court" of Article III could have played anything like the role it has in containing the energies of our people within the framework of a civilized and civilizing jurisprudence.

The Supreme Court itself has, of course, been an object of great attention, scholarly and otherwise, and the meaning it has for the quality of American life has been assayed at length.[14] That it should have been created at all was not a question that needed to be explored, since its existence is, as I have said, inseparable from the grant of a national judicial power. The historical origins of the inferior federal courts are important, however, inasmuch as their creation did not flow inexorably from the grant. And yet the effort and ingenuity expended to reconstruct these origins and to divine the reasons underlying the decision taken seem something less than commensurate with what, in the event, has proved to be the practical significance of that decision.

There are two other circumstances which suggest a lower level of appreciative assessment than may be deserved. One is our failure in general to recommend a like decision to new and emerging states cast in a federalist framework. No less an expert and devoted observer of the national judicial power than Professor Paul Freund of the Harvard Law School had this to say in 1954 when he wrote on the lessons for the budding European Economic Community of our experience of a federal judiciary:

> A Supreme Court, it is assumed, will be provided for in the Constitution. The establishment of inferior federal tribunals, it is suggested, may best be left to the legislature, under a grant of power for this purpose in the Constitution. While several federal constitutions have authorized a full system of inferior federal courts, only in the United States has such a parallel system been actually established. In view of the expense involved, as well as possible duplication and confusion of jurisdiction as between these federal courts and the state courts, the burden is on those who would favor such a scheme.[15]

Canada happens to be one of those countries which has a basic charter authorizing the establishment of inferior federal courts,[16] but which has never done so. The *New York Times* of January 2, 1967, carried a long piece of self-appraisal of their government by Canadians as they opened the centennial year. This is what it had to say about the courts:

> The Supreme Court is a virtually unknown body whose decisions have no finality about them. Jean Lesage, while Premier of Quebec, announced he would

ignore any court ruling against Quebec's claim to oil under the Gulf of St. Lawrence.

Premier Bennett did not wait for the high court's ruling, due in February, to announce last month that British Columbia owned everything under the Pacific Ocean as far out as the continental shelf.

.   .   .   .

The point might be argued in law school debates, but an Ottawa lawyer asserted recently that Canada at centennial time struggles with a weak confederation system resembling that discarded by the United States in 1789. Instead of the central government growing stronger as in the United States, in Canada it is the other way around.[17]

Whatever else may be said of the United States Supreme Court, it is neither unknown nor ignored. Is it perhaps possible that its effectiveness depends in some considerable degree upon the supporting structure of inferior federal courts; and that, in contrast, the Supreme Court of Canada lives in lofty impotence because it has no comparable underpinning? Canadians lamenting the insignificance of their federal judicial power may be tempted to re-examine the disuse of the discretion given them by their organic Act to establish inferior federal courts.

The second circumstance intimating a certain inattention to the decision to establish lower federal courts is a failure to identify those passages in our history when the availability of such courts has been of critical importance. Much has been made of the role played by the lower federal courts in the giving of aid and comfort to commercial and industrial interests straining for fulfillment in the young and growing nation. Without the assurance of fair treatment in the resolution of disputes and the honoring of undertakings, which these courts provided, the freedom and burgeoning of trade envisioned by the Commerce Clause would never have come to pass. But the more dramatic instances of this essentiality are of a later time and, because they are concerned with less material values, are perhaps rightly to be regarded as of a higher order in the scale of human achievement.

Brown v. Board of Education will be long remembered as the first formidable command post established by the Supreme Court in the battle against racial discrimination in the public schools.[18] But it is interesting to speculate as to what options the Supreme Court would have had if it had remained the one—and the only—court invested with the federal judicial power. It will be recalled that the Court gave its ruling on the merits in May of 1954, but that it asked for further arguments on the issue of relief and did not speak to this highly practical side of the controversy until May of 1955. At that time it remanded the cases to the District Courts, making it clear that these courts were to be the primary instrumentalities for the effectuation of the broad principles the Supreme Court had announced.[19]

The promulgation of those principles would have provided an infinitely more daunting prospect in the absence of the machinery provided by the inferior federal courts. Their performance in the discharge of this difficult task has been less than even, but is it conceivable that the job could have been entrusted entirely to the state courts, bearing in mind the differences in loyalties and the vulnerability to local pressures inherent in an elective system of judges? The federal judges themselves have, even with the security provided them by the Constitution, found the going hard. It is not fanciful to think that it would have been too much for unsheltered state judges, given the intelligence and integrity of which their federal brothers assuredly have no monopoly. Certainly it would have been hard to have asked them to risk such an exposure with so few shields.

It is, thus, no detraction from the Supreme Court's achievement in the school desegregation cases to conclude that its path was made easier, its range of alternatives enlarged, by decisions taken earlier in the life of the republic with respect to the organization of national judicial power. The same can be said of many other advancements and alterations in legal doctrine summoned into being by the Supreme Court's expansive reading of familiar constitutional phrases. The implementation of the Court's strictures upon the malapportionment of voting power involves great complexities of a largely administrative nature.[20] Without the availability of the local federal courts, it is difficult to believe that this audacious venture by the Supreme Court into the political thickets would have appeared feasible in the first place. The extraordinary degree of tangible success which has characterized that foray may again be credited in substantial part to the tact and judgment of the many less exalted federal judges who have been obliged to effectuate the new doctrines at the grass roots. As in the case of school desegregation, it is hard to believe that things would have gone as well with only state trial and appellate courts to carry out the federal requirements.

The list could be multiplied. An innovating step by the Supreme Court in the field of criminal procedure, laying down new standards to be observed in the administration of state and federal criminal justice alike,[21] is taken with the reassurance that federal trial courts are open throughout the land to entertain claims that the new rights have been disregarded. If the advances in this area be generally deemed of an improving nature, then this accretion to our developing mosaic of a good society is also a dividend of wise judicial organization. Legislative committees disposed to be autocratic in the conduct of their hearings and investigations,[22] and holders of executive authority who appoint themselves censors of the lives and thoughts of private citizens—[23] these, too, have had to reckon with the knowledge that disregard of Supreme Court doctrine is likely to be ventilated promptly in the United States District Court down the street before a judge whose loyalty is to the document that guarantees his independence.

Since no court may in its decision-making be oblivious of the degree to which its word will be made good,[24] the inescapable effect of these judicial arrangements is to give the Supreme Court a wider scope in which to function. If one believes, as I do, that over time and in the large the Court has sustained and invigorated the ideals underlying the federal union, then there should be due recognition of anything which enlarges its range of effective choice.

The Fundamental Determinations

A backward look at the initial creation and organization of the national judicial power appears at this point to be in order for two purposes. One is for the purely historical interest of observing how easily we might have taken our place among the federalisms whose judicial power has found inadequate fulfillment through the medium of "one supreme Court." [25] The other—and infinitely more important—is to lay a background against which there can be a more informed and meaningful speculation about the shape of judicial organization in the future. We are, under the spur of new issues and the advancing avalanche of litigation, perhaps on the threshold of determinations in this area as fateful as those faced in 1787 by the architects of the new nation. It is at least interesting, and perhaps reassuring, to examine the degree to which it was given them to see as through a glass, darkly.[26]

The framers of the Constitution at Philadelphia do not appear to have entertained any doubts of the desirability of investing the new government with a judicial power. That there should be "one supreme Court" appears not even to have been debated. But the contending Randolph and Paterson blueprints diverged immediately upon the issue of inferior federal courts. The former, which contemplated their creation, prevailed at first, but subsequent motions for reconsideration, and consequent elimination, of this feature of the plan were carried. The voting margin being narrow, the classic conditions of compromise were evident; and the conflicting positions were adjusted by authorizing Congress to provide lower federal courts if and when it should see fit to do so.

The level of the floor debate at the Convention on this

issue seems, in retrospect, lacking in sensitivity to the importance of the subject matter. It was urged, for example, that lower federal courts would involve a substantial expense, as burdensome as it was unnecessary in view of the availability of the state courts. When one looks today at the ratio of the federal judicial expense to the budget of the federal establishment as a whole,[27] this argument has a flavor of triviality. But even so prescient a statesman as James Madison was content to cast his defense in the small change of administrative convenience, asserting that "appeals would be multiplied to an oppressive degree" if the state courts were relied upon as the courts of first instance in every case.[28]

Only Edmund Randolph is reported as having moved closely toward the core of the more exalted issues of policy. John Rutledge had asserted that "the State tribunals might and ought to be left in all cases to decide in the first instance, the right of appeal to the Supreme National Tribunal being sufficient to secure the National rights and uniformity of judgments"; that to create lower federal courts would make "an unnecessary encroachment on the jurisdiction of the States and [create] unnecessary obstacles to their adoption of the new system." [29] Randolph, contrarily, argued that the matters at stake were too fundamental to the health of the new nation to turn on tactical considerations in the future fight for ratification. His point of departure was "that the Courts of the States cannot be trusted with the administration of the National laws. The objects of jurisdiction are such as will often place the general and local policy at variance." [30] Whether or not his proposal was the right or only one, Randolph was, in the parlance of advocacy, talking to the point.

The Constitution, as has been said, committed the issue to the wisdom of the legislative branch, which was not slow to act. One of the early actions of the First Congress was, in the Judiciary Act of 1789,[31] to exercise its grant of discretion in favor of lower federal courts. How much the soil of this decision had been cultivated by the two intervening years of ratification debate is far from clear. Many of the strongest backers of the new charter purported to believe that what Congress might decide to do under this power was not especially important. Edmund Pendleton told the Virginia ratifying convention that he thought it "highly probable that [Congress's] first experiment will be to appoint the State Courts to have the inferior Federal jurisdiction." [32] James Madison opined that he, too, thought this was what Congress would do, at least "when they find the tribunals of the States established on a good footing." [33] A pro-Constitution correspondent of James Monroe made this response to an appeal for support:

I think it would be wise to institute the State Courts, where they are well established, as the inferior Courts, for should the United States erect separate Courts, the probability is that bickerings will arise between the two jurisdictions; this, as you say, is in the discretion of Congress; and I trust that that discretion will be exercised properly.[34]

These expressions are, of course, subject to the impeachment that perhaps they were intended to play down the importance of the issue pending ratification. But there seems to have been no such conscious purpose, as witness the fact that Alexander Hamilton, pressing hard for ratification by any and every means, in Federalist No. 81 went beyond a mere defense of the Convention's relegation of the issue to Congress and spoke to the merits of creating lower federal courts. Defending the Constitutional provision on the ground that it was a necessary legal foundation for state court handling of federal matters if Congress should make that choice, in the next breath he aggressively queried the wisdom of such a utilization of the discretion afforded. He thought popular confidence in state court handling would be diminished because, as he put it, "the most discerning cannot foresee how far the prevalency of a local spirit may be found to disqualify the local tribunals for the jurisdiction of national causes. . . ." State court judges without life tenure would, he said, be "too little independent to be relied upon for an inflexible execution of the national laws."[35] Since, in his view, the facilitation or limitation of appeal rights should vary with the degree of trust reposed in trial courts by the people at large, a Congressional decision to employ state courts must necessarily entail the most liberal provision for appeals, with inevitable envelopment of the one federal court which could hear and decide them.

As in the case of the Constitution, the handiwork of the First Congress in the judicial field was characterized by compromise. Those who opposed the creation of any lower federal courts at all failed of their objective. But it was also true that disappointment was the portion of those who wanted to see such courts entrusted with the full sweep of the judicial power contemplated by Article III. It has been suggested that, on balance, it was the latter who felt the greater chagrin at the final result,[36] but the meager historical record does not dictate this conclusion.

The Senate took the initiative with respect to the preparation and enactment of a judiciary bill. A select committee was chosen to take this business in hand, and half of its number had served in the Philadelphia Convention. Its chairman, Oliver Ellsworth, early described its proposals as involving the creation of a District Court with one judge resident in each state having a jurisdiction confined largely to admiralty cases, and a Circuit

Court composed of the District Judge and two Supreme Court Justices with jurisdiction to try cases between foreigners and citizens, and between citizens of different states.[37] This description accurately prefigured the final form of the bill, and it is noteworthy that it did not commit to these inferior federal courts the full range of jurisdictional subjects identified in Article III. The significant omission, of course, relates to cases arising under the Constitution, laws, and treaties of the United States.

The debates of the Senate at the time the bill was considered were both closed to the public and unrecorded; but it seems likely that there was opposition to the creation of lower federal courts even with this restricted jurisdiction. In the House of Representatives, we know that this was so. A prominent member of the House, Fisher Ames, said of the pending judiciary bill in a letter to a friend: "The question whether we shall have inferior federal tribunals (except Admiralty Courts, which were not denied to be necessary) was very formidably contested."[38] Since there appears to have been general agreement that maritime matters required some kind of inferior federal courts, it may be said that the dispute was cast in terms of the grants of jurisdiction to be made to such courts as were established.

It could be argued, from the language of Article III, that any inferior federal courts, once created, automatically were vested with all of the jurisdiction referred to in Article III, except those matters reserved to the original jurisdiction of the Supreme Court. The precise words are that the judicial power of the United States "shall be vested in one supreme Court and such inferior Courts as the Congress may from time to time ordain and establish," and that that power extends "to all cases in law and equity arising under the Constitution, the Laws of the United States, and Treaties made . . . under their Authority. . . ." Thus it could be said that, once Congress decides to bring an inferior court into being, the Constitution itself endows that court with the complete jurisdictional range of the federal judicial power. So respectable an authority as Joseph Story always believed this to be true, and that the Congressional discretion in jurisdictional matters was limited to the making of exceptions and regulations in respect of the appellate jurisdiction of the Supreme Court.[39]

That view did not prevail, either in the First Congress or thereafter; and it has become an accepted article of our constitutional faith that the lower federal courts exercise the jurisdiction given them by Congress—no more and no other. What the scope of that jurisdiction should be at any one point in time is a question of public policy for Congress to explore and to resolve. The question before the First Congress, then, was essentially that of whether an inferior federal court created to handle admiralty matters should be given any other judicial business of the kind comprehended within the national judicial power.

In the House of Representatives a serious effort was made to answer this question in the negative. A motion was made to restrict the lower federal courts to admiralty matters alone; and it was upon the disposition of this motion that the fate of those courts hung. The proponents of the motion took common ground upon the availability of the state court systems and their authority to deal in the first instance with claims or defenses derived from federal sources. To the extent that such courts would prove to be mistaken or niggardly in their recognition of such rights, the "one supreme Court" created by Article III would be able to supply correction upon appeal. It was pointed out that state court judges were under the direct admonition of the Constitution to observe the supremacy of federal law, and that it was not to be assumed lightly that this command would be ignored. On the few occasions that it might be, there was the saving relief of appeal to a supreme federal tribunal. "Such an arrangement," it was said, "would save immense expense, would occasion little innovation in the ancient forms of judicial proceedings amongst the people, and would also, without difficulty, accommodate jury trials, in matters of fact, to the wishes of each State, as every one would retain its own usage." [40]

The battle lines did not form upon purely geographical lines: A New Hampshire man said that he looked upon the plan with "horror" because it was "a foundation laid for discord, civil wars, and all its concomitants."[41] A South Carolinian, by contrast, thought the bill did not go far enough in its investiture of the proposed lower federal courts with the constitutional heads of jurisdiction.[42]

It is important to remember that the bill under debate did not purport to exhaust the jurisdictional alternatives of Article III, notably in the matter of general federal question jurisdiction. What it did do, among other things, was to entrust to the new courts suits between citizens of different states. It was the necessity for this grant that principally engaged the attention of the debaters of the bill; and it is well to remember that the generalizations they summoned to their aid are to be read in the context of this proposal.

Thus in James Madison's assertion to the House that a review of state court systems "will satisfy us that they cannot be trusted with the execution of the Federal laws,"[43] it is not so clear that he is sounding a broader theme than when he said to the Virginia ratifying convention that "It may happen that a strong prejudice may arise in some states, against the citizens of others, who may have claims against them. We know that tardy, and even defective administration of justice has happened in some states."[44] What remains inconclusive from the deliberations of the First Congress is the degree to which its original establishment of the lower federal courts was prompted by a conscious vision that they were needed for reasons going far beyond the assurance of justice on a nondiscriminatory basis to the nonresident suitor.

Historical research with respect to the initial organization of the national judicial power has been in large part the handmaiden of advocacy of the merits or demerits of eliminating or reducing diversity jurisdiction. Those who favor such a course argue that the xenophobia of an earlier day, even if it existed,[45] is not the mark of the present, and that a jurisdiction conferred as a protection against it need not be continued.[46] Their opponents insist that diversity jurisdiction should continue because a mere absence of bias in a state court is not a guarantee of competence, and that this latter quality is more likely to be found in the lower federal courts than in their state counterparts.[47]

What is either absent or obscure in the historical record of 1787–89 is any accurate prevision of the large purposes which would be served by the inferior federal courts in the years to come. It was almost as if, having recognized that maritime jurisdiction necessitated some new courts, it was thought that they might as well be available also for diversity cases in order to assure equal treatment to nonresident litigants. There is little, if any, articulation of the function which lower federal courts could play in creating a corpus of uniform national law on subjects of country-wide significance, or in generally serving as a bulwark for the wide-ranging exertion by Congress and the President of the broad grants of power to each contained in the Constitution. There is certainly no explicit speculation about the degree to which an active and innovating Supreme Court might need the supporting services of lower federal courts in order to make its commands effective.

The Allocation of Jurisdiction

For those who wish to see the national judicial power actively in the service of national interests and purposes, the key clause of Article III is the one extending that power "to all Cases, in Law and Equity, arising under this Constitution, the Laws of the United States, and Treaties made, or which shall be made, under their Authority." To those of our generation—whose lives have coincided with a spectacular expansion of federal authority—it always comes as something of a surprise that our ancestors were so slow to commit this jurisdiction to the federal courts. Except for one early abortive attempt to do so by an enfeebled and rejected Federalist Party,[48] more than three-quarters of a century went by before

Congress took this step. Until 1875 the federal courts were, except for admiralty, largely "subsidiary courts," serving no national purpose other than to provide a sanctuary for nonresident litigants from local prejudice.[49]

The Judiciary Act [50] passed by Congress in that year, however, floated upon a tide of nationalizing sentiment flooding from the successful suppression of the Confederacy. In the judicial field its first signs had appeared during the war years themselves, and had thereafter accelerated as Congress moved to protect federal officer and freedman alike against hostile local treatment. The culminating step in 1875 of clothing the lower federal courts with federal question jurisdiction appears to have been taken as a matter of course and in the absence, either within or without the halls of Congress, of any serious or lengthy debate or discussion. Its leading historians have said of this legislative judgment that "sensitiveness to 'states' rights', fear of rivalry with state courts and respect for state sentiment, were swept aside by the great impulse of national feeling born of the Civil War." [51]

It was a critical decision for the future of the federal courts. It provided the sinews by which those courts became powerful instruments for the centralizing and unifying tendencies of a national law. It created the essential conditions under which the federal courts could give judicial expression to the strong federal leadership provided by presidents like Wilson and the two Roosevelts. It anticipated, in a very real if perhaps unintended sense, the New Freedom and the New Deal, and the two great world wars. It put the federal judiciary into the main stream of a tradition of federal response to a widening area of human problems inviting the exertion of governmental power.

However far the Congressional vision of 1875 may have penetrated into the mists of the future—and there is little evidence that it was directed anywhere but at the immediate past—it is not likely that it embraced two major developments in the law. One is the remarkable extent to which the common law pattern of judge-made law has been eroded by the ubiquity of statutes providing rules of decision. The other is the growing importance of the Constitution itself as a source of both substantive law and procedural requirements.

In the case of the former, the trend is not confined to the federal establishment. The state legislatures have, in varying degrees, emulated Congress in the escalation of their output. Between them, large areas have been insulated from judicial creativity in the common law tradition, except as the inevitable ellipses and ambiguities of the written word provide scope for imaginative judicial interpretation. State and federal judges alike work today under a lowering cloud cover of statutory prescription.[52]

The second, however, is much more of a purely federal phenomenon. Although there are doubtless instances where the words of a state constitution have been given enlarged or unexpected content by a state supreme court, with profound impact upon the corpus of existing state law, it is the United States Constitution which has been the notable beneficiary or victim, depending upon the point of view, of the transforming effect of the adventurous accommodation by the Supreme Court of old phrases to new times. It is in the area of constitutional interpretation that the ancient concept of judicial finding and declaring of the law is now finding its amplest opportunity for fulfillment. To the extent that the Supreme Court, as constituted at any one point in time, finds that concept congenial, the probabilities are greatly enhanced that the number of cases "arising under the Constitution" for handling by the lower federal courts will increase spectacularly.

We need not stop to speculate as to whether, or how much, these developments were foreseen in 1875. What is of more immediate consequence to the cause of wise and efficient organization of judicial power is how far it is given to us today to see the road ahead. What offers an apparent contrast between the two points in time nearly one hundred years apart is the confident mood of affirmation of national power following the Civil War, as compared with the present doubts that salvation lies only in a federal solution and with the present disposition to seek deliverance in a turning away from extreme centralization in governmental structure and authority.

This is not to suggest that there is likely to be any lessening of the role of the Constitution as a source of law, or that Congress will not continue freely to utilize its legislative powers. Neither is there to be anticipated any slackening in the need for extensive employment of the federal judicial power to assert the supremacy of federal law and to assure its uniformity and comprehensibility. The new mood does not envisage a federal rejection of responsibility, but a rational sharing of it, to the end that the total resources available are put to the most efficient use.

The demands upon the total quantum of judicial power—federal and state—are presently growing without seeming limit, and they bid fair to be as novel in nature as they are endless in number. Those demands will be satisfied, and the strains they impose surmounted, only by wise and imaginative organization of that power in both its aspects.

I I

The Stresses
of Coexistence

As LONG AGO AS 1868—and in the congenial climate of a rising tide of sentiment for the vigorous assertion of national power—the Supreme Court observed that "the preservation of the States, and the maintenance of their governments, are as much within the design and care of the Constitution as the preservation of the Union and the maintenance of the National government." [1] Less than a hundred years later, however, dissatisfaction in state judicial circles with the observance of this principle culminated in drastic proposals for constitutional revision to create a "Court of the Union" which would redress the alleged intolerable encroachments upon state judicial power by the federal.[2] That those proposals were lacking in any very broad base of popular feeling is attested by their failure to command effective support. That they were made at all, however, suggests that stress and strain are inevitable when judicial power is organized along parallel lines.

This condition of conflict is the inescapable consequence, human nature being what it is, of the inclusion of the Supremacy Clause in the Constitution of 1787.[3] In a partnership, no one relishes the subordinate role. Moreover, where the dominant power impinges upon interests as distinctly identified and as earnestly conceived as are those in the care of state sovereignty, it is small wonder that "nothing could inspire resentment to shriller tones of invective, than the fact that . . . the national Constitution and laws to which the states must be subjected can be nothing else than the national Constitution and laws as interpreted by the national tribunal entrusted with this task of supervision, even though that interpretation may in some particular case not be the one arrived at, or even passionately held, by the dominant interest in the affected state." [4]

The Supremacy Clause, however essential to the viability of a federal union, was pregnant from the very beginning with the seeds of discord. Conflict was only made more certain by the establishment of lower federal courts scattered throughout the land and committed to the same obligation as the "one supreme Court," the declaring and enforcing of an overriding national law. The pricks of higher authority are felt only the more keenly when they come from familiars in the courthouse across the street who happen to hold a judicial commission signed in Washington.

At least one eloquent voice on the Supreme Court has labored mightily and with great good will to allay the tensions between state and national judicial power. Justice William J. Brennan, with an unimpeachable background of many distinguished years of service as a state trial and appellate judge, has affirmed to his former colleagues that "there is no justification for the view that we are headed in opposite directions, and that the only legal bond between us is the subjugating one of the supremacy clause." His reconciling thesis is that the total law of our federalism has two components, and that, although in a dual system of court organization "federal courts decide questions of state law, and state courts ones of federal law," it always remains true that "each tribunal is supreme in its own field, and in the final analysis neither can do the other's job." His reassurance of continuing dignity and vitality in the state courts is based on the fact that the state courts persist in having "the duty of rendering the final decision on the overwhelming majority of the controversies in this country which end up as cases in court." [5]

A state court judge might rejoin that who actually decides a case is less important than the source of the law that must be applied in making the decision; and that the imbalance, if such there be, between state and federal judicial power derives from the expanding range of federal law as the binding rule to be applied. The creative latitude which a state court judge feels should be his right in dealing with the controversies traditionally committed to his care is circumscribed to the extent that the fashioning of state substantive and procedural law must be carried on in the shadow of burgeoning federal doctrine. A marked trend towards such enlargement of federal law may be as sound in the national interest as it is inevitable in the society taking shape about us; my purpose for the moment, however, is not to weigh the merits of such a development, but to identify it as one of the factors generating friction in a judicial system organized as ours presently is.

Federal Common Law

The phenomenon can be more or less neatly labelled a new federal common law. The characterization "new" may be less faithful to history than is strictly warranted, but the adjective is useful in denoting that there have been visible variations in the life cycle of this legal concept. The idea was not, for example, born with the new federal courts. The national judicial power founded in 1787 was so strongly conceived of as incidental to a federal government of expressly limited powers and purposes that the notion of its roaming at large in the law-making tradition of the English common law courts was wholly alien. The Supreme Court early decreed that there could be no federal common law of crimes, that no one could be prosecuted and punished under federal authority for any conduct except that which Congress, acting always within the confines of its own enumerated powers, has explicitly made criminal.[6] That doctrine persists to the present day, although Congress has steadily enlarged the kinds of conduct which it has denominated as criminal.[7]

It was not until the dual system was some decades old that the lower federal courts were told by the Supreme Court that, over and beyond their admiralty jurisdiction, theirs was a creative power to discover and declare in diversity cases substantive rules of decision in the area of general commercial law. Thus, in *Swift v. Tyson*,[8] Justice Story, in a characteristic burst of nationalistic enthusiasm for the law-making needs and capacities of the federal courts, marked out an area of federal common law in which a federal judge could decide cases without reference to the judge-made precedents of the state in which he sat.

As we all know, *Swift v. Tyson* survived more than fifty years beyond the time when the federal courts were given a truly national law-making function by the grant of federal question jurisdiction. Although there was at least one scholarly rumbling in the interim as to the propriety of this demotion of state law,[9] correction did not come until 1938, when the Supreme Court, to the surprise of the parties involved, intruded the issue into an otherwise routine lawsuit by the name of *Erie R.R. v. Tompkins*.[10] Bending to Mr. Justice Brandeis' deeply felt consciousness of error, it held that Story had pointed the Court down a path of iniquity of constitutional proportions. In diversity cases, said the Court, involving as they do no element of federal interest, it is the law of the state that governs, including that part of it created by the state judges alone.

In what it has become fashionable in some quarters to regard as a long history of ever-widening federal encroachment, *Erie* stands as at least one instance of a voluntary relinquishment by the federal courts of power long assumed at the expense of the states. It could not but contribute to a sense of increased importance, responsibility, and self-esteem on the part of the state judiciary. In the perennially uneasy interplay of feelings between state and national authority, this perhaps had in itself some intangible values, if one believes that it is never healthy in a federalism for one sovereignty to swallow up the others.

Erie has had its critics from the first; their strictures crescendoed with the Supreme Court's strong reaffirmation of its "outcome-determinative" principle in *Guaranty Trust Co. v. York*,[11] and moderated somewhat with the ambivalent note sounded in *Byrd v. Blue Ridge Rural Electric Cooperative*.[12] *Erie* has offered many difficulties in implementation because of the often unclear and indecisive face presented by the applicable state law. Its principal justification continues to be the anomalies inherent in a situation where the same lawsuits come out differently by reason of the accidents of residence of the parties. This alone imposed a considerable strain upon the acceptability of a dual court system.

Thirty years after *Erie* ended one era of federal common law, the focus of attention is very much upon what is termed to be a "new" one. Those who follow the fortunes of a dual court system are again trying to assess the degree to which effective judicial law-making is centering in the federal judges as compared with their state-court counterparts, elevating the influence of the one and depressing that of the other, and causing the resolution of more and more litigations to turn upon the content of a corpus of federal non-statutory law determined by the federal courts without reference to, and frequently in conflict with, the rules declared by the state courts. The latter profess to wonder whether what was given them by *Erie* is being taken away by some of its successors.[13]

If this is in fact the case, it might be expected that the derogators of *Erie* would be loudest in their praise of this new departure. Although their devotion to all things federal would presumably cause them to view it with satisfaction, the warmest welcome has been extended by *Erie's* most eloquent defender. Judge Henry Friendly, in his notable Cardozo Lecture of 1964,[14] set himself the seemingly paradoxical task of praising both at the same time. His thesis on the first branch of his subject was that the goal of uniformity sought by Justice Story in *Swift v. Tyson* was as spurious in original conception as it proved to be in practice, and that the general common law it sanctified upset the allocation of law-making power between state and federal court envisaged by the Constitution. The new, or specialized, federal common law, as he called it by way of rhetorical contrast with that condemned in *Erie*, had already exhibited a genuine capacity to achieve unity in judicial decision in all courts, state and federal—a capacity solidly and constitutionally founded upon the Supremacy Clause. In the psychiatric idiom which today has even penetrated sober legal discussion, Judge Friendly remarked that "having rid itself of subconscious feelings of guilt for federal poaching on state preserves, the Supreme Court became freer to insist on deference to federal decisions by the states where deference was due." [15]

For those who may be apprehensive about the impact of the new federal common law on the reach and authority of state law, the possibility of restraints generated by self-induced guilt complexes in Supreme Court Justices may seem a vain hope indeed. They wish to see more clearly than they can now the kinds of boundaries which the federal courts will set for themselves in their resort to a common law of their own making, as distinct from the laws of the state having a substantial relation to the transaction in suit. They also want to know what considerations will appear relevant to a federal court confronted with a choice between available state-created legal principles and those to be devised by itself with a view to protecting a federal interest assumed to be significant. It is not easy to do either of these at present. One acute authority has recently concluded that, although it is certain that the federal courts have unmistakably set themselves the exercise of propounding a federal common law, "no clear principles have yet emerged from the cases so that little may be done other than to present examples of cases in which the problem was faced. . . . They reveal a variety of approaches to the problem." [16]

In one of its latest cases in this field, the Supreme Court did make clear that the whole concept of a federal common law is rooted in conflict—a discernible incompatibility between some national interest of importance and the rule of state law which would normally apply. Thus, it said, "in deciding whether rules of federal common law should be fashioned, normally the guiding principle is that a significant conflict between some federal policy or interest and the use of state law in the premises must first be specifically shown." [17] Where such a conflict has been demonstrated, the Court has not deferred to general state law, even in such areas as immemorially associated therewith as contract formation [18] and title to physical property.[19] Many cases have appeared that accept a significant federal interest in the law surrounding government contracts and securities, where the federal government itself is affected by the outcome.[20] The necessity to the federal government today of prompt and efficient realization of the taxes it imposes is reflected in a greater readiness to construct a body of federal law appropriate to that end.[21] Additionally, we have had a reasonably clear signal that, where general law doctrines are relevant or decisive in the resolution of suits involving the conduct of our foreign relations, those doctrines will be shaped in federal, and not in state, courts.[22]

These are enough to suggest that there is a great potential for the subordination of state to federal law, and the dangers of disaffection to the fabric of federalism are correspondingly great. The solvent of statesmanship on the part of the senior partner will be sorely needed if animosities are to be minimized and the state courts are not to feel themselves the objects of a demeaning neglect and a cavalier dismissal. It is here that the standards to be employed by the federal courts in appraising the necessity to invoke a common law of their own will be so important.

The omens in this regard are encouraging. The Supreme Court has rejected some efforts to seek a federal rule of decision simply because a transaction has some federal aspect; [23] and it has said that, even when there is a ponderable federal interest, there must still be put in the balance against it such factors as the strength of the interest of the state in having its own rules govern, and the practical feasibility of the creation by a federal judge of a substitute for the state rule.[24] Not least in this respect is the evidence that the Supreme Court will not assume that, because Congress could have created a statutory rule of decision if it had wanted to, a federal court must fashion one at all events.[25] Where this last is done in the presence of a Congressional indication that it be done, its friendly and understanding reception at the level of state interest is an infinitely greater probability.

Pre-emption

In addition to the emerging concept of a federal common law, there is another principle which operates to shrink the area in which state law can function. This is the idea of pre-emption. Broadly stated, the doctrine is that, where Congress has legislated with regard to a particular subject matter, the Congressional intention, even though not expressed, is that the states are to exercise neither their legislative nor their judicial power in the same field. It is, of course, the federal courts who have the last word in divining such an intention and interposing it as a bar to state action. The assumption of such a power by the federal courts is, needless to say, a potentially rich source of friction between the two legal systems.[26]

When the Supreme Court, in the fear-ridden decade of the 1950's so poisoned by the late Senator McCarthy, declared that Pennsylvania could not take criminal action against alleged subversives because Congress did not intend that it should,[27] there was a violent reaction from self-styled preservers of our federalist form of government. What was overlooked, in particular, on this occasion was that the Pennsylvania Supreme Court first reached this result in its own view of the matter,[28] and, in general, that, if the United States Supreme Court had so grossly misread the Congressional purpose, the Congress, in which the people of Pennsylvania and all other states were represented, could swiftly and speedily correct the mistake. But these obvious facts did not quiet the chorus of complaint that the state policies embodied in state laws had been improperly subordinated by the federal judiciary. And it has not entirely subsided even after the Court not long thereafter discerned some room for state action against political subversion,[29] and after the country generally began to move away from McCarthyism to more adult concerns.

A more far-reaching circumscription, by means of pre-emption, of state law-making and administering power in a vastly more important area has taken place in the field of labor relations. In *San Diego Building Trades Council v. Garmon*,[30] the Supreme Court recognized and initiated a major limitation upon the capacity of state legislatures and courts to deal with relations between employer and worker in an industrial society. This has extended to the interpretation and enforcement of contracts reached between the two. In the *Lincoln Mills* case,[31] the Supreme Court held that the grant of jurisdiction to federal courts over suits based upon collective bargaining agreements was a Congressional mandate for the fashioning of a federal common law of labor contracts; and that, even where such suits were brought in state courts, it was that law which must be observed. In this respect, at least, the preemption and federal common law principles have coalesced to relegate to virtual extinction a familiar and long-established area of state law formulation.

Judge Friendly has speculated that *Lincoln Mills* perhaps portends further significant incursions by federal judicial law-making into preserves once presided over completely and authoritatively by state law. Since corporations can only come into being by state consent and on state-imposed conditions, it has long been true that state law governs questions of stockholders' rights and management responsibilities. But, as Congress addresses itself more and more to the regulation of securities issuance and trading and the solicitation of proxies, it may, as he says, be inevitable that a uniform federal common law of corporations will take shape at the hands of the federal courts, perhaps as much for the objective of making nation-wide corporate enterprises viable vis-à-vis unrealistic state requirements as for the elevation of state standards of conduct which may in some cases be considered too undemanding.[32]

Whether one views prospects of this kind with satisfaction in terms of their potential for greater certainty and uniformity in the ascertainment of applicable law, or with sadness over their supplanting of the states' law-making function, it seems clear that change and flux are the order of the day in the functioning of the state and federal judiciaries. And, since change in established relationships is never wholly comfortable or easily accepted, we can be sure that the shifting boundaries of law-making power inherent in such phenomena as pre-emption and a new federal common law will generate their tensions in the structure of federalism.

Standards of Criminal Justice

The loudest discords have sounded in the field of criminal law and procedure. This is not surprising. In the first place, one of the important areas commonly accepted as being reserved to the states is the prosecution and punishment of crime. The federal law of crimes is wholly statutory, and is confined to those special classes of conduct which affect or are incidental to the legislative powers vested in Congress by the Constitution. The more familiar offenses of murder, robbery, rape, housebreaking, assault, and so on are all within the scope of state authority and responsibility. The mere enumeration of these crimes suggests that they are of the character which most actively agitates the popular mind in the immediate environment of their commission; their handling provokes strong emotional reactions which not infrequently find expression in political terms. This supplies a second reason why federal interference produces resentment.

A clash was inevitable from the day the Fourteenth Amendment became part of the Constitution.[33] The rights thereby recognized as secured against state action made it certain that federal claims would be advanced in state criminal cases, the disposition of which would ultimately be determined by the Supreme Court. Furthermore, the writ of habeas corpus was always available as a means of pursuing in the federal courts a claim of federal right which a state court had ignored or incorrectly resolved.[34] The reach of federal habeas corpus has been steadily lengthening by reason of the Supreme Court's ever-widening translation of the specific guarantees of the national Bill of Rights into the more generalized limitations upon state action stated in the Fourteenth Amendment. There is no need here to identify the particular steps in that process, or to debate the historical accuracy of the assumptions which have been made as to the purposes of the authors of the federal protections. Even if the detailed specification in the national charter were absent, it seems inevitable that an expanding concept of the notions of ordered liberty implicit in the Fourteenth Amendment standard of due process of law would have brought the same result.

As has been so perceptively pointed out by a reasoned
voice intimately associated with this Law School—Justice Schaefer of the Illinois Supreme Court—this
concept serves significant national objectives extending
beyond our geographical borders.[35] If, as he hypothe-
sizes, one appropriate measure of the level of our
civilization is the degree of fairness achieved in our administration of criminal justice, then our influence with
foreign observers depends in no small part upon our at-
tainments in this respect. It is important, however, that
the bright face we offer to the outside world in this regard be not tarnished by unnecessary disharmony at
home among those with overlapping functions and responsibilities in the operation of the dual legal system.
The conflict and discontent have, unhappily, been
plainly evident, even to those who view it from without,
and the dissatisfaction has centered about the role of
federal habeas corpus.

The relevant federal statute is Section 2254 of Title 28
of the United States Code. It provides that state prisoners
may not pursue federal habeas corpus relief unless they
have exhausted the remedies provided to the same end in
the state courts, or unless no such remedies are effectively available to them.[36] In *Brown v. Allen*,[37] the Supreme Court held that the fact of exhaustion did not
conclude the matter, and that federal claims must still be
entertained and resolved by the federal courts. This de-

cision brought into sharp focus the mounting resentment within the states of close federal monitoring of state criminal justice. It was the federal judges themselves, interestingly enough, who moved most determinedly to blunt the thrust of *Brown v. Allen*. The Judicial Conference of the United States approved and transmitted to Congress a bill [38] to enlarge Section 2254 by providing that no federal judge could entertain a habeas corpus petition from a state prisoner unless it presented a substantial federal constitutional issue not theretofore raised and determined under fair and adequate state procedures available for that purpose, or which could not thereafter be so raised and determined with opportunity for Supreme Court review. In submitting the proposal, its purpose was characterized by the Conference as "to eliminate the delays and interferences with the State criminal law and the consequent resentment on the part of judges of the several States which have arisen through the review by habeas corpus in the lower Federal courts of the judgments of State courts." [39]

The witness designated by the Judicial Conference to present to Congress the case for the bill was Chief Judge Parker of the Fourth Circuit, whose many years of distinguished service upon the federal bench were not marked by any lack of devotion to the assertion of federal supremacy in appropriate spheres. He said the bill might properly be termed one "to restrain the abuse of habeas corpus in the lower Federal courts by prisoners who have been convicted in State courts and who seek to have the action of the State courts reviewed and reversed by the lower Federal courts." [40] He asserted that habeas corpus was never intended to enable federal district courts to sit in appellate judgment upon the actions of state courts, including the highest courts in those systems. He insisted that Section 2254 in its existing form was intended to put an end to that practice, and that only through misconceived judicial interpretation had it failed to do so. The strength of his feelings in the matter are indicated by this summation of his Congressional testimony:

> . . . We have two systems of courts in this country, the State courts and the Federal courts, and as a Federal judge I want to say I think the State courts are entitled to great respect. I think by and large the State courts are just as able as the Federal courts and just as conscientious. When the State courts have convicted a man, it was the opinion of the Conference that if inquiry is to be made as to his conviction it should be done in the State courts if possible and make a record that could be reviewed by the Supreme Court of the United States. In some States it is not possible to do that, and in those States he can go to the Federal court. [41]

5 5

Whether the Congress did not accept Judge Parker's assumptions about the equivalence in competence of state and federal judges, or whether it thought the proposition was sufficiently dubious to make it unsafe to assume that an already overburdened Supreme Court could, by itself and without the help of the inferior federal courts, put to rights every neglect or misconception of federal constitutional claims occurring in the manifold state systems, the bill did not become law.[42] Indeed, two more recent Supreme Court decisions, *Fay v. Noia* [43] and *Townsend v. Sain*,[44] have placed added emphasis upon the necessity of great scope for the vindication in the federal courts of federal claims put forward by state prisoners. One has construed Section 2254 as contemplating that the state remedy be available as of the time of the federal challenge and not earlier, and the other has insisted upon the duty of the federal courts in habeas corpus to explore anew the findings of fact made in state proceedings.

The sense of injury in the states persists, and the volume of federal habeas corpus cases continues to grow.[45] Whatever the merits of the matter may be, the point for the moment is that the organization of judicial power along its present lines has caused a clamorous cacophony,[46] as unseemly in aspect as it is fraught with serious questions about the efficiency of the current allocation and utilization of our already over-extended store of judicial resources.

Inter-court Interference

As unsettling as it is for state courts to conduct criminal proceedings under the shadow of the collateral impeachment afforded by habeas corpus in the lower federal courts, the interference is not direct. That possibility does obtain, however, and in both civil and criminal proceedings, where judicial power is so organized that courts of separate sovereignties exist side by side, theoretically capable of issuing commands to each other or to the parties seeking to proceed in either. This is the problem generally subsumed under the subject of the powers of one court to restrain the institution or continuance of legal proceedings in another. It is a problem which has contributed to the frictions inherent in our fully developed dual system of courts.[47]

In exploring this source of conflict, a separation must be made at the outset between what may be termed its federal-state and its state-federal aspects. The broad equity powers reposed in both the state and federal courts have traditionally been regarded as enabling each to enjoin litigation in another tribunal within its own system.

Thus, a state court may prevent parties before it from proceeding in another state court, either in the same or a different state. In the same way, a federal court can limit resort to another federal court, either in the same district or outside. When, however, the interaction is between a state and a federal court, the definition of power must take into account considerations deriving from the independent origins and status of the two courts.

As early as 1793, the Congress of the United States took heed of the danger to federal-state relations implicit in the capacity of the newly created federal courts to interfere with state proceedings. It passed a statute forbidding federal courts from granting injunctions "to stay proceedings in any court of a state." [48] The courts themselves, however, were quick to note that the language of the law appeared to be limited to proceedings already under way, as distinguished from those not yet begun. And over the years there also grew up a number of judicially conceived exceptions to the legislative fiat.[49] In 1941 the Supreme Court at last appeared to think that this process had gone too far; and, in *Toucey v. New York Life Ins. Co.*,[50] it acted to turn the tide. In doing so, it largely purported to give effect to what it considered to be indications of a Congressional solicitude for the delicacies of the distribution of judicial power between the dual systems of courts.

The Congressional response to this decision in 1948

was hardly in keeping with the Court's assumptions. It produced Section 2283 of Title 28 of the United States Code, which reiterated the ban on federal injunctions against the continuance of state court proceedings, but with three explicit exceptions, i.e., where "expressly authorized by Act of Congress, or where necessary in aid of . . . jurisdiction, or to protect or effectuate [the issuing court's] judgments." [51] The new statute was characterized by its authors as intended to restore "the basic law as generally understood and interpreted prior to the *Toucey* decision." [52] It has been accurately remarked, however, that "since there were pre-*Toucey* exceptions that do not seem to come within the language of the revised section, and since the law prior to *Toucey* was by no means well defined and consistently applied, the scope of the present federal injunctive power is not nearly as clear as the revisers seem to have expected." [53]

In 1955 the Supreme Court hailed the revised statute as "continuing evidence of confidence in the state courts, reinforced by a desire to avoid direct conflicts between state and federal courts." [54] Ten years later, however, the Court in *Dombrowski v. Pfister* [55] directed the District Court to enjoin impending state criminal prosecutions under a state anti-subversive activities statute which the Court believed to have a chilling effect upon rights of free speech guaranteed by the First Amendment. The Court noted in a brief reference that Section 2283 did not stand in its way since the anti-injunction aspect of that statute has always been regarded as inoperative until state proceedings have actually been instituted. But its unwillingness to remit the individual concerned to the state criminal courts, even though his federal defenses could there be asserted and ultimately vindicated, if need be, on Supreme Court review, suggests that the Court, in this instance at any rate, had neither confidence in the state courts involved nor any overwhelming desire to avoid conflict with them. Whether it would have felt insuperably impeded by the statute if the state had moved a little faster remains uncertain, as does the present state of the law generally with respect to federal-state injunctions. That uncertainty, if anything, only compounds the tensions latent in this situation of lower federal courts armed with large, albeit imprecisely understood, powers to act directly against the hearing and disposition by a state court of a lawsuit within its jurisdiction.

The American Law Institute, in its current *Study of the Division of Jurisdiction Between State and Federal Courts,* has taken note of this difficulty, and has recognized not only that some statutory restriction is desirable in the interest of federal-state relations, but also that any such statute should be "as clear as the subject matter, and the variety of possible problems which may arise under it, will permit." [56] To this end it has formulated a further revision of Section 2283 which, with one exception, continues the differentiation between state proceedings in being and those not yet instituted. This one exception reflects generally the *Dombrowski* circumstances: It permits a federal injunction to restrain a state criminal prosecution that "should not be permitted to continue either because the statute or other law that is the basis of the prosecution plainly cannot constitutionally be applied . . . or because the prosecution is so plainly discriminatory against one who has engaged in conduct privileged under the Constitution or laws of the United States as to amount to a denial of the equal protection of the laws." [57]

This was acceptable to as representative a group as the membership of the Institute,[58] and presumably few other fair-minded citizens would quarrel with it. It is, nonetheless, a ponderable departure from the principle that state courts can be relied upon to discern and to enforce the commands of the supreme national law. As *Dombrowski* itself had its roots in southern animosities over the race issue, so the ALI exception is an example of how the backwardness of a few states in the legal accommodation of racial equality results in the formulation of legal rules in terms applicable to all. In law, as elsewhere, the lowest common denominator affects the statement of the norm, and raises the spectre that it may be applied in a situation for which it was never actually intended. So it is that deterioration in so-called states' rights is frequently attributable to those who profess the loudest concern for them.

Turning to the second aspect of the direct interference problem, that is to say, the enjoining of federal suits by the state courts, the materials for discussion are much more scanty. We start with the fact that the Constitution is silent on the subject and Congress has never legislated with reference to it. Neither has any state legislature purported to prescribe the powers or prohibitions of its own courts on this score. Perhaps because state courts have so rarely attempted to impose limitations upon federal proceedings, it has been the fashion to suppose that such power does not exist, although this is far from being a necessary conclusion.[59] Since the general equity powers of the state courts are essentially the same as those possessed by the lower federal courts, they presumably have, as a general proposition, a similar scope. This approach is certainly the most appealing in its connotations for a federalism which thrives best in a climate of mutual respect. Certainly where Congress has identified particular exceptions in which its courts are free to bring their equity powers to bear against state proceedings, it would seem both politic and fair to concede to the state courts a like capacity.

The Supreme Court has not, however, appeared to be so minded. One of its few pronouncements in this field is

recent in point of time—*Donovan v. City of Dallas* [60]—
and is not characterized by any apparent generosity towards the principle of reciprocity. Indeed, the Court
appears to have palpably recoiled from the idea that state
courts can enjoin federal proceedings for the same reasons that federal courts can enjoin state proceedings. It
preferred to analyze the problem in narrow and restric-
tive jurisdictional terms, and to ignore the considerations
which clothe courts, state and federal alike, with general
equitable powers. It has been argued with some force
that the Court, in its newly conceived passion for enun-
ciating general law, could construct "a common law of
state-federal injunctions," leaving to Congress the task of
imposing by statute such alterations as it might, from
time to time, think compelled by policy considerations
which it perceives more plainly than the Court, "somewhat as it has done in the converse case of federal-state
injunctions." [61] It is hard to quarrel with the conclusion
that a course of this kind would be more consonant with
the play there should always be in the joints of a dual
system of courts.

This is the approach which has commended itself to
the reporters directing the American Law Institute's
inquiry into federal jurisdiction. They propose a federal
statute paralleling Section 2283 that premises a general
prohibition upon state court injunctions against federal
proceedings or the enforcement of federal judgments,

subject to two specific exceptions. These are founded upon the necessity to protect (1) the issuing court's jurisdiction over property in its custody or under its control, and (2) against vexatious and harassing relitigation of matters already determined by the issuing court in a civil action. The first is said to be grounded in the present case law, and the other—presumably in response to *Donovan*—to be an alteration of it.[62]

Although such a statute falls short of full reciprocity in this area, it embodies in substantial degree the general proposition that "state courts should be able to enjoin federal court proceedings whenever, in the converse situation, a federal court could enjoin proceedings before a state court," which proposition is said to rest in turn upon the fact that "any concept of the state courts as 'inferior courts' has been repeatedly and rightly rejected." [63]

The Concept of Abstention

There is a final category of cases not involving direct attempts by federal or state courts to interfere with proceedings in the other but which have imposed substantial strains upon federal-state relationships. Early in the nation's history the adoption of the Eleventh

Amendment [64] appeared to put to rest the answerability of the sovereign states to suit in the federal courts. But in 1908 the Supreme Court purported to see a distinction between a suit against a state *eo nomine*, on the one hand, and, on the other, an action against state officials acting under color of state legislative or executive authority which itself is claimed to be in conflict with rights guaranteed by the Constitution. In the latter instance it was ruled that federal jurisdiction attaches and, if the claims of constitutional right are demonstrated, the officer-defendants can be restrained from carrying out their apparent responsibilities. [65]

In an era of corporate and commercial enterprise steadily becoming more nation-wide in scope, this decision was certain to assure collision with such vital state concerns as revenue-raising and economic regulation. State tax collection and the enforcement of regulatory statutes were directly impeded and frustrated by injunctions issued by federal district judges, frequently by reference to a substantive concept of Fourteenth Amendment due process having a highly economic content. [66] The states were in effect denied even the right of having these debatable issues determined first in the more congenial and understanding atmosphere of their own courts where it was less likely that the implementation of state policies would be stymied pending ultimate resolution of the issues in the United States Supreme Court.

Congress took some account of the sense of injury felt by the states, and a number of statutory ameliorations were made. One was the requirement that the enjoining federal district courts act through three judges rather than one, thereby reducing somewhat the dangers of state programs being blocked by the crotchets and personal predilections of a single individual.[67] A second was a prohibition upon federal court interference with state tax collection where the state itself provided "plain, speedy, and efficient" procedures for raising the federal issues in the state courts.[68] And a like restraint was commanded with respect to the utilization of federal court suits to attack state orders addressed to the rates of those offering public utility services.[69]

These expedients, obviously, went only part of the way, and their implicit recognition of the gravity of the strain perhaps only had the consequence of exacerbating it. Over and above the mandatory restrictions imposed by Congress upon freewheeling federal trial courts, the Supreme Court endeavored to exert an emollient influence through the exercise of its supervisory powers over its less exalted brethren. It variously and from time to time asserted that the exercise of federal jurisdiction should be conditioned upon a showing that state administrative avenues of relief had been fully pursued, and that, on occasion, the district courts should, in the interest of avoiding a clash between state and federal authority, simply decline a jurisdiction otherwise evident. Short of this closing the doors to the federal courthouse completely, the Court evolved the notion of sending the federal suitor across the street to the state court, temporarily, for the purpose of getting a determination of issues of state law relevant to the ultimate resolution of the case. This was the doctrine of abstention.[70]

First articulated most clearly for the Court by Justice Frankfurter in 1941, *Railroad Commission v. Pullman Co.,*[71] abstention has had a checkered career, and its present state is frail indeed. Its essential rationale was that federal jurisdiction was not denied but merely postponed. Its advantage for the federal court was that difficult constitutional issues might never have to be decided, and that the confusion inevitably attendant upon conflicting answers by state and federal courts to concededly state issues could be avoided. It was thought to allay the federal-state tensions inherent in the coordinate judicial powers by its graceful recognition of the primacy of the state courts in the definition of state law, and by its minimizing the chances that state programs would be thwarted at their inception by federal intercession.

The coin proved, however, to have another side. This was the interminable delay in the eventual disposition of the lawsuit. In two notable instances, seven years was required before the federal claimant received a final answer.[72] In addition to the expense that delays of this order entailed, there was the brooding uncertainty of long-pending litigation which frays the nerves of the litigants and defaces the image of justice in the sight of the public. Even costs of this magnitude might be deemed bearable if there were certainty that they were outweighed by a thorough-going relaxation in federal-state friction, but it has been far from clear that abstention has contributed much to the achievement of this end. The federal trial courts have undoubtedly been relieved of the burden of a few cases, since it appears that some lawsuits remitted to the state courts under abstention have never returned, either because the litigants became exhausted or because the federal claim was ultimately established in direct review by the Supreme Court.[73] But it is at least questionable whether, in these times of crowded dockets everywhere, state susceptibilities are soothed by a mere transfer of case loads.

The Supreme Court, in any event, appears largely to have written off this experiment in greater accommodation of the twin judicial structures. The last eight times abstention has gone to the Supreme Court well, it has come back empty-handed.[74] If the Court has not rejected its creature for good and all, there is an unmistakable element of jaundice in its current view of it as operating "to require piecemeal adjudication in many courts . . . thereby delaying ultimate adjudication on the merits for an undue length of time." [75] Perhaps it cannot be said that the doctrine is dead, but its prospects as a continuing solvent of federalism are dim indeed, in the absence of any successful attack on the problem of delay.

There is at least one visible manifestation of a continuing interest on the part of the states in abstention. The Commissioners on Uniform State Laws have been working on a Uniform Certification of Questions of Law Act;[76] and the legislatures of four states have acted to empower their courts to hear and to decide issues of state law certified to them by federal tribunals.[77] The thought is that provision for this kind of direct reference will so facilitate the giving of answers by the state courts to state law questions as to make the delay in federal court disposition tolerable. And so it might be if a federal district court, upon identifying a relevant state law issue which has not been clearly or authoritatively resolved by the state judicial system, could submit that issue directly to the highest court of the state and receive an answer back with reasonable dispatch. It was this potentiality for expedition that caused the American Law Institute to include in its proposals a provision under which any federal court may, if it chooses, certify a controlling question of state law to the highest court of the state in question under a procedure established by the state for that purpose. Such a certification must be premised, however, upon an express finding that it "will not cause undue delay or be prejudicial to the parties." [78]

In addition to certification, the ALI proposes the continuance of a discretionary power in the district courts to abstain under fairly rigorous conditions. It has been noted that the ALI's approach in this regard is more analogous to a relinquishment of jurisdiction than to a mere postponement of its exercise, and one which is therefore more responsive to a policy of minimizing friction between the two systems.[79] This seems borne out by the shape of the ALI plan, wherein a district court may stay a suit before it in which federal jurisdiction plainly exists, but which also "presents issues of State law which ought to be determined in a State proceeding. . . ." To grant such a stay, however, the court must first find four things: (1) state law is unclear as to the issues in question, (2) there is reason to think that resolution of a federal constitutional issue may be avoided or that there is a danger of impeding the effectuation of state policies by a federal guess about state law which may prove wrong, (3) a plain, speedy, and efficient remedy is available in the state courts, and (4) federal claims, including relevant factual issues, can be adequately protected by ultimate Supreme Court review. A stay once granted may be vacated at any time if the state proceeding fails to achieve an early and effective determination of the state issue. Unless the stay is vacated, however, the federal suit is to proceed no further, and the rightness of the state court determination is left to direct review by the Supreme Court.[80]

Whether these ALI proposals, or spreading adoption by state legislatures of certification procedures, will breathe new life into the seemingly moribund device of abstention is hard to say. They do represent earnest efforts to adjust potential frictions in the coexistence of federal and state judicial power, and my interest in them at the moment is not so much in their merit as in their recognition of the reality of conflict.

This catalogue is not complete. There are other aspects of the strain which might be listed. But, hopefully, the point has been adequately made that, in the field of judicial power as in executive and legislative, federalism has its problems of accommodation, demonstrably increased by the decision of long ago to establish a system of inferior federal courts. These problems remind one that, in the ripeness of advanced age, Thomas Jefferson found one of the prime virtues of the Constitution to be the scope it afforded for avoidance of direct confrontation between state and national power. But, he said, the partisans of each must prudently observe "the line of demarcation" from a distance, instead "of rashly overleaping it, or throwing grapples ahead to haul to hereafter." [81]

III

The Quest
for Accommodation

THE PROBLEMS THROWN UP by the shape of life in the closing third of the twentieth century—domestic and international, social, economic, and even physical survival in an increasingly contaminated and crowded environment—are imposing great strains on our existing institutions of government. Periodic doubts have been expressed about the capacity of the legislative process to respond to these urgencies. President Kennedy, as he approached the end of his first term, is said to have been given to somber speculations about the very viability of the office of the Presidency under the many burdens it is called upon to sustain. The judiciary has not been exempt from these forebodings. One long-time observer of the American scene has sagely remarked that the judicial structure "sometimes seems to be buckling under the strain of administering justice under the same law to half a dozen civilizations." [1]

This last is very much worth thinking about. This country—of continental proportions in geographical scope and of infinite diversity in the ethnic, economic, and educational status of its citizens—does present a sometimes bewildering array of cultures and subcultures. The rural South and the northern cities are not the same. Los Angeles is not New York. The cool and calculating practitioner of organized crime is not the young public school drop-out who assaults passers-by on the streets in the hope of getting a few dollars. The income tax evader or the antitrust violator is not the man who is goaded into criminal violence by the strains of family living or other emotional relationships. The narcotics addict, the chronic alcoholic, the prostitute, and the homosexual do not fit easily into the criminal law.[2] Yet we maintain the fiction that the courts must apply legal rules of universal application; and we have done very little as yet to formulate meaningful and sensible differentiations between these highly divergent circumstances.

The law of libel is a good example. Long regarded as a matter of state law, the Supreme Court concluded that it must protect a national newspaper like the *New York Times* from vengeful and racially backward Southern courts and juries.[3] To warrant this intercession it had to turn to the Constitution. The constitutional principle it formulated to this end must, by definition, have nation-wide applicability. There is, however, little realistic re-semblance between an Alabama libel suit against the *Times* in a racially-inflamed context, and an action by a minor public official in New Hampshire against his al-leged defamers.[4] But our tradition of the even-handed application of law requires the same result, despite the absence in the latter case of all those sinister factors below the surface of the pleadings which obviously im-pelled the initial enunciation of this new reading of the Constitution.

Another aspect of the crisis conditions faced by the state and federal courts is the sheer volume of litigation, both trial and appellate.[5] There are many contributing causes to this phenomenon. One is the simple fact that the long-continued period of affluence for some seg-ments of our society permits increasing indulgence of the expensive luxury of litigation. Well-heeled clients press their attorneys not only to take their disputes into court but, further, to go as high in the judicial hierarchy as the law permits in order to try to reverse an initially unfavorable result. The tax laws encourage this by the deductions of litigation costs which are frequently al-lowed.[6] The bar itself seems to offer less resistance than formerly to their clients' insistence upon pursuing ill-conceived claims and hopeless appeals. There was a time when a responsible practitioner carefully nursed his professional standing with the Supreme Court by refusing to file unlikely *certiorari* petitions, thinking thereby to be assured of serious consideration when he did elect to act. Those who must breast the current flood of filings [7] detect fewer and fewer instances of such restraint; and every appellate court sees each day direct appeals which any competent lawyer knows must prove unavailing.

The criminal law has to be distinguished in this regard. The ever-widening scope of the provision of counsel to indigent defendants, at public or private expense, means that appointed lawyers have little choice, if they are not to be made to defend themselves later on collateral attack against charges of constitutionally ineffective assistance, but to exhaust all possible legal avenues to their clients' freedom, no matter how unpromising. And it is in the criminal field that both trial and appellate courts are under mounting pressures of sheer volume. Of the 68 cases pending on the Supreme Court's appellate docket when it first convened in the 1967 term, nearly 35% were criminal. In my own circuit, there are some 1200 felony cases pending for trial in the District Court. In the federal district courts generally, the criminal volume has climbed to above 25%; [8] and, since it is the state courts rather than the federal who are chiefly concerned with crime, these statistics are eloquently suggestive of what is happening there. It is plainly evident that we must, as a nation, get on with the preventive business of attacking crime at its roots, or we must resign ourselves to the inevitability of allocating more of our resources to the administration of criminal justice.

There is, finally, the fact that expanding constitutional concepts like equal protection and due process are causing people to turn more and more to the courts for relief against alleged oppressions, both by the public authorities and by their fellow citizens. Mention has been made of the impact of these concepts in the criminal field, but there is a comparable development in the civil. This enlargement of constitutional rights has been accompanied more recently by the spectacularly increased availability of civil legal aid to the poor. Many communities have struggled valiantly for decades to raise by voluntary giving the funds necessary to provide legal assistance for the civil concerns of those who cannot afford to pay lawyers. But no one involved in those efforts has ever deluded himself by thinking that there has ever been more than surface penetration of the problem. Although it has long been plain that many among us have had tremendous unmet needs for medical and educational help, perhaps an even larger deficit has accumulated in the legal area. Many people with means go through their entire lives without seeking the legal advice they need, but infinitely more have had neither the means nor the awareness to bring the law to bear upon the problems of daily living.

The federal government's anti-poverty program may be far from realizing many of its objectives, but it appears to have wrought a major extension of the scope of civil legal aid. The current Congressional appropriations for neighborhood legal services already dwarf the annual expenditures heretofore possible from charitable giving; [9] and this infusion of new money and new talent is bringing to the courts legal issues which otherwise would have remained dormant. Recently some public officials in California raised their voices in complaint about the unsettling effects of the activities of the California Rural Legal Assistance program, functioning under the auspices of the Federal Office of Economic Opportunity. This program has nine different offices scattered throughout California's agricultural regions. A responsible attorney-participant in the program was quoted as saying that the outcry was caused because "we are opening legal issues never raised before, and some of these involve public agencies." [10] Typical of those issues, and of the 700 cases handled by one of the nine offices alone in the first year of its existence, was a due process challenge to a justice court requirement that a woman against whom a merchant had gotten a judgment for an unpaid bill of $140 had to put up $140 in court as a condition of appeal. A second example was an attack upon the authority of the state to revoke a driver's license—so essential to many employment opportunities—without a finding of fault. Local welfare departments throughout the country are finding that their clients are being backed up by legal advice in the complaints they make of administration; and the general dissatisfaction with this area is emphasized by a spate of lawsuits in which long-standing rules and practices are being questioned and, with increasing frequency, invalidated.[11]

The boy expelled from West Point on the eve of graduation hales the Secretary of the Army into court.[12] The soldier who does not want to go to Vietnam files a suit.[13] The dedicated believer in church-state separation asks a court to order the Postmaster General not to put a portrait of the Madonna on a postage stamp.[14] The prison inmate who doesn't like the food writes out a habeas corpus petition,[15] as does also the mental hospital patient who wants out or who disagrees with the form of therapy he is receiving.[16] The Third Circuit recently had to deal with the claim of a law professor who characterized a law review's rejection of his article as state action denying the equal protection of the laws.[17] And court clerks' offices around the nation are bulging with taxpayers' complaints that their elected representatives in the legislature and the executive are not performing as they should. Time was when the citizen aggrieved by some aspect of prevailing public policy was wont to say, "there ought to be a law." Now he warns, "I'll see you in court."

This all implies a deepening disillusionment with both the efficacy and the speed of achieving reform through direct political action, by appeals to legislators or to executive officeholders backed up by the threat of the vote. The mood seems to be to seek relief immediately in court and not to wait for the next election. Although many thoughtful—and by no means illiberal—persons have sober reservations about this transfer of political action from the ballot box to the courts, there is little evidence that the ordinary citizen is unduly perturbed about judicial intervention. He rather appears to like the idea that there is one branch of the government which can and will deal quickly and effectively with shortcomings in the laws or obtuseness in their administration. This may conceivably not be in the long-range interest of a democratic society organized on the assumptions underlying our own, but the courts are confronted with the short-range problem of skyrocketing dockets and the new and novel issues intruded upon their attention. There must be a continuing and intensive inquiry, therefore, into whether the present organization of judicial power, and the concomitant utilization of judicial resources, is best suited to the dimensions of the demands currently being made upon them.

One thing is clear. So long as the total quantum of judicial power is organized in the form of a dual system of state and federal courts structurally paralleling each other from top to bottom, clash and conflict should be minimized between these partners in the task of dispatching the total amount of judicial business. As in the founding days of the republic, so now the proposal periodically recurs that there should be only one set of trial courts in which all issues, state and federal, could be raised and decided in the first instance. If the task of reviewing questions of federal law be regarded as too great for the "one supreme Court" provided in the Constitution, as it undoubtedly is, then it is suggested that that Court be aided by a number of regional federal courts of appeals to which federal questions could be brought from the state sysems. If the state systems were made the courts of original jurisdiction, then, it is said, the problems created by federal district courts sitting in the midst of state courts could be eliminated.[18]

The idea is far from absurd. But what it probably founders upon for the foreseeable future is the great variation in the quality of state judicial systems, with their diverse, but mainly backward, provisions for judicial selection and tenure. New York, for example, has recently had a convention to write a new state constitution. Initiated with high hopes that its work might signal a concentrically widening resurgence of effective state government, it came up with a new Judicial Article which failed utterly to move toward a significant improvement in judicial selection and tenure. If New York, a bellwether in the area of good state government, can do no better than this, the millennium in this regard is scarcely at hand. The more likely prospect is that the state courts will go on much as they do now, with slow steps here and there towards judicial reform, and occasionally a major breakthrough, as happened in New Jersey over 20 years ago and in Illinois in 1962. But, in the large, they are not at the moment able to serve as the nation's only trial courts and thereby to render the federal district courts unnecessary.

Jurisdiction Re-examined

It does not follow, however, that there can be no redistribution of jurisdiction between the state and federal courts. Chief Justice Warren, in his annual appearance before the American Law Institute in 1959, invited a careful and comprehensive inquiry into that very matter. His central purpose was stated in these words:

It is essential that we achieve a proper jurisdictional balance between the federal and state court systems, assigning to each system those cases most appropriate in the light of the basic principles of federalism.[19]

The Institute has made a major response to that challenge in its *Study of the Division of Jurisdiction Between State and Federal Courts.* That *Study* has addressed itself separately to the two main areas of federal jurisdiction—diversity and federal question. In the case of the former, it has made proposals which would, it is estimated, result in a net reduction of about 50% in the existing number of diversity cases in the federal district courts.[20] In the matter of federal question jurisdiction, it has, on balance, significantly enlarged the opportunities of the citizen to have his claims of federal right first heard and determined by federal judges.[21]

The premises underlying these conclusions seem to me unassailable. First, with regard to diversity, when the apparent reason for the original grant (i.e., the danger of unfair preferment of local litigants over their out-of-state opponents) has long since ceased to exist, at least a start can be made on reducing that grant's scope.[22] With respect to federal question jurisdiction, uniformity and expertness in the application of federal law seem more likely to accrue, at least at the present time, from resolutions of that law in the federal courts.[23] The interaction between the two is that, with mounting volumes of all kinds of cases, the crucial importance of correct determination of federal claims emphasizes the desirability of relieving the federal courts of suits lacking that importance.

The diversity proposals, although adopted by the membership of the Institute,[24] have drawn fire from both within and without that body. The posture of the opponents seems essentially to be that it was a happy accident that the founders, anticipating a need to shield outsiders from local bias, created diversity jurisdiction. Whether or not that need in fact existed originally or has receded over the years to the point of extinction, there should be no relinquishment because the federal courts are better places to try lawsuits of any kind than state courts. They offer, so it is said, better judges, better juries, better procedures, better facilities; and no working lawyer in his right mind would wish to see any diminution of the opportunity to try his cases in the federal courts.[25]

This position is not grounded in any principle relevant to federalism, except as some of its proponents seem to say that an all-embracing federal government is, and should be, the wave of the future. More among its backers appear to be successful members of the bar who make states' rights speeches by night but want to try their cases by day in the federal courts, and who, therefore, make of professional interest and convenience a standard for the allocation of jurisdiction between the dual systems. Although it is possible to understand, and even to sympathize with, the motivations giving rise to it, as a standard it is largely devoid of rationality, except as it is assumed that decay and decline of state government are ends in themselves. Furthermore, it takes from behind the cause of state judicial reform an impetus which could be of the greatest consequence: namely, the pressure upon local leaders of the bar to fight for improvement of the courts in which they must represent their most important clients.

These practitioners apart, it is hard to see why anyone concerned to have the federal courts in the best position to perform their vital functions of making federal law and protecting federal rights, particularly of the disadvantaged, should resist the Institute's diversity proposals. They seem to me a realistic recognition that all our judicial resources, state and federal, are going to be needed to cope with rising tides of litigation, and that a rational distribution of that load is essential. An allocation which causes cases deriving from state law to be tried in state courts is rational; the objection to it, that some state courts are not as good as federal courts, is of a different order. The answer to that objection is not to abandon reasoned jurisdictional principles but, by their very adoption, to make such principles powerful engines for state judicial reform.

Of course, if one believes that all law should be of a

federal provenance, then there is no reason, by present remissions of jurisdiction from federal to state courts, to delay the day when state courts can be dispensed with completely. But this approach would seem to be at odds with the second thoughts many admirers of the federal establishment are having about extreme centralization in governmental authority and function. Perhaps these doubts are ill-conceived in their entirety, or do not extend to judicial authority and function, as distinct from legislative and executive. But it is by no means clear that Congress and the federal judges should be the sole source of law. In law-making, as elsewhere, there are merits in dispersion.

One example comes to mind. Auto accident litigation is very likely the greatest single threat today to the viability of the courts, at least on the civil side. It is widely believed that there must be some fundamental change in the methods of resolving these disputes, in order to remove their clogging effect from the courts. Many studies have been made, and many suggestions have been forthcoming; [26] what is needed now is for the comparative merits of these alternatives to be tested in actual practice, in order that informed choices may be made among them. It seems likely that some one or more of the 50 states is on the point of making an effort along one of these lines.[27] From these coordinate experimental laboratories, as Brandeis called them, may well come the materials of a national solution devoid of the dangers of national action based solely upon hypothesis and conjecture. It could not be so if the states atrophy completely as sources of law.

No one views the infinite and indiscriminate proliferation of judges as the true solution of the litigation explosion. The machinery for the administration of justice does not get better solely because it becomes bigger. Judges are not wiser for being more numerous. We are on the threshold of new ways of doing things in the judicial field, and a sustained period of trail and error is, and ought to be, on our legal horizons. There is talk of complete pretrial discovery as a way to get faster, as well as fairer, disposition of criminal cases.[28] In England, juries have all but disappeared in civil cases, and 1967 marks the beginning in that country of less than unanimous verdicts in criminal trials.[29] Our traditional assumption of the necessity of at least one direct appeal in every case is being questioned.[30] These ideas, and others like them, require the testing of actual use before their merits can finally and confidently be determined. The state courts, in all their variety, offer an extraordinary opportunity in this respect which cannot be found in the uniformity of the federal system.

The ALI's proposals on diversity jurisdiction would, thus, augment the grist for these mills by turning back to the state courts a substantial number of cases which turn upon state law. With respect to federal question jurisdiction, their thrust is in the other direction. Mainly by removing the present monetary limitations upon the assertion of federal claims by plaintiffs, and by permitting defendants with federal defenses to remove actions from state to federal courts, the Institute would increase the number of cases cognizable in the federal courts. The principal justification for this is that uniformity is especially essential in the determination and application of federal law. The further premise is that uniformity is more likely to obtain within a single system of courts manned by judges who are likely to have both greater understanding of, and greater hospitality toward, the sources of federal law.[31]

There has, as yet, been little vocal opposition to the direction being taken by the ALI in the federal question area. This is due, I believe, only in part to the force of the uniformity rationale. It is also attributable to a more intangible factor; and that is a broadening popular recognition and acceptance of the availability of the federal courts as the vindicator of the intensely personal rights of the citizen guaranteed him by the Constitution. Growing numbers of people take comfort in the thought that the federal district court is at hand to protect them against local oppressions by the application of a law which does not derive from local *mores* and institutions. The time was when the federal district courts seemed to be preoccupied with suits brought by large foreign corporations to disrupt local regulatory efforts of an economic nature. Today it is the local resident of slender means and less influence who looks upon the federal district court as the bulwark against interference by his neighbors or his immediate government with the rights he enjoys in common with all his countrymen from coast to coast. People of all races and economic levels appear to take satisfaction in the presence among them of this security structure. Although most of them will have no occasion to invoke its offices, it is good to know that it is there.

The expansion of federal question jurisdiction in the federal courts does not, of course, necessarily entail contraction of the power of state courts to deal with the same cases, provided the adversaries are content to have their disputes adjudicated there. The federal right involved always has the assurance of ultimate review in the United States Supreme Court. Over time, and as state court systems are progressively strengthened and modernized, it may well be that more and more people will be content to rely upon state tribunals for informed and intelligent consideration of their claims of federal right. The greater number and wider geographic accessibility of state courts make this a consummation devoutly to be wished. The ALI proposals place no impediments in the path of steady movement in that direction and, indeed, in their totality are calculated to give impetus to it. There is no reason why a competent and independent state judiciary cannot do full justice to federal rights, rendering invariable resort to the federal courts unnecessary. When that day arrives, our judicial resources will be at their maximum of efficient utilization, and the liberties of our citizens will be enjoying their greatest security.

There is one particular in which trials in state and federal courts are presenting an increasingly common aspect. The greatest procedural advancement of our time was the promulgation of the Federal Rules of Civil Procedure in 1938. The impact of those Rules has not been on the federal system alone. They have, in addition, provided a model for state procedural improvement. In many states they have been taken over virtually intact,[32] and their influence is plainly discernible everywhere, so much so that it is indeed far from fanciful to suppose that, sooner rather than later, we may achieve substantial identity between the dual systems of courts in the procedural field. This is one area in which state-oriented lawyers, teachers, and judges have enthusiastically welcomed innovations of federal origin.[33]

Federal rule-making has not been content to rest on the laurels of 1938. We now have Federal Rules of Criminal Procedure and of Appellate Procedure. Federal Rules of Evidence are in preparation. Federal rule-making has been characterized both by venturesome expansion into new fields, and by constant reexamination and improvement of rules already in effect. The whole process has been marked by willingness to consider and to draw upon state experience where devices developed in the state courts have promise for the federal system. The spirit of tolerance and cooperation which has pervaded this field has visibly eased the stresses of coexistence, and holds out the future promise of a uniform practice in both sets of courts. The eventual achievement of that goal would be an important breach in the barriers between them.

The Administrative Alternative

Any discussion of the accommodation of overlapping judicial powers must take into account the prospect that means other than courts may be employed to deal with emerging problems. Where judicial power is not relied upon at all as an instrument of government, we need not be concerned with its fragmentation. It is likely that imaginative adaptation of the principle of insurance may eliminate a vast amount of litigation in the torts field. The ferment in the auto accident area is, in the long view, perhaps only a taste of what is to come. A final elimination of poverty through a negative income tax or one of the other schemes for a minimum family allowance [34] could have a significant effect upon the volume of litigation, especially in the welfare field, with which courts are becoming more and more preoccupied. But, as the Social Security System has spawned its own legal issues for judicial resolution, the disappearance of sub-standard economic existence will not bring the millennium of a society wholly lacking in disputes requiring peaceful resolution through law. What is possible is that courtroom adversary litigation, as we have known it, may prove to be a less desirable means of achieving such resolution.

That, of course, will depend to a large degree upon the nature of the problem. But some of the problems that seem certain to pre-empt our most urgent attention in the years ahead do not, perhaps, lend themselves effectively to solution by judicial power. There is, for example, the question of a water supply which, if not diminishing absolutely, is being exposed by a growing population and new industrial needs to a demand which results in a relative shrinkage. As is always true where a fundamental necessity is in short supply, lawsuits abound, but it is by no means certain that their termination in judicial victory for one side or the other can do more for the abiding water problem than make it worse. One view is that natural resource problems of this kind are handled best at the local level, where the peculiar physical characteristics are best understood; and that what is needed is for the state courts, particularly in those states controlling large water supplies, to conceive and apply enlightened legal principles which can in themselves be regarded as the equivalent of a national policy for water conservation and allocation.[35] Others have asserted the desirability of a cooperative effort on the part of federal and state governments, cast in the form of regional compacts to which the national government will be a party. Any such compact would presumably provide its own machinery for dispute settling, which might or might not have a place for the courts.[36]

A third school regards this second alternative as only slightly less obsolete than the first. It thinks that the worsening water problem is only compounded by the fashioning of water law in lawsuits asserting either private or public rights. The water problem is a tissue of technical, social, and political issues which have left court-constructed doctrines of water law far behind, and which are not best suited for fresh exploration within the familiar confines of the judicial trial. The proponents of this view see salvation only in unrelieved federal control, exerted through an administrative agency with powers that partake of each of the triad of executive, legislative, and judicial. Under this approach there is little, if any, occasion to worry about jurisdictional divisions between state and federal courts, or conflicts between them, because neither will have any role in shaping the legal rules for water.[37]

Water seeks its levels without relation to political boundary lines. It moves by its own laws and neither knowing nor caring whether it has gone from city to suburb, or state to state. It is this geographically regional setting of the legal problems which makes them intractable in terms of purely judicial resolution, at least by the dual system of courts as presently constituted. But this is a feature the water problem has markedly in common with many of the other major concerns which press insistently for our attention and action—air pollution, mass transportation, power supply, aesthetic deterioration—to name but a few which are generating a sense of panic among those who live in the massive metropolitan areas. As we have, in some of these, already turned in large part to the administration of law through the independent agency with nation-wide jurisdiction, so is it not improbable that the administrative process is likely to experience another great leap forward. A common, or even a statutory, law of nuisance applied in the courts is arguably no substitute for an expert agency armed with investigative, rule-making, and adjudicative powers, and whose authority is unconstricted by state, city, and county dividing lines.

A generation ago lawyers and judges spent a lot of time deploring "the new despotism" and wondering darkly whether the very existence of the courts was not being threatened by the phenomenon of administrative law. The answer given at that time was to tighten up the procedures of the agencies, and to emphasize the availability of judicial review. In the latter case, there is some question whether the intervening years have dispelled all the fears that mandatory court review of agency action can be a needless cultivation of judicial sensitivities which gives judges not only a reason for being but also a chance to effectuate their public policy opinions in some highly important areas of American life where their special competence is not readily apparent.

To the extent that an agency is acting counter to the policies intended to be embodied in the statute creating it, it might be thought that sufficient assurance against despotism resides in the availability of continuing supervision by the legislature, and that judicial review is not needed for this purpose. As increasingly critical assignments are made to nonjudicial agencies, it may be supposed that correspondingly higher standards of personnel selection and stronger guarantees of independence for those chosen will be forthcoming. With better people at all agency levels, it should be possible, by a well-conceived system of internal appellate review, to satisfy the popular feeling that some appeal to a higher level is an inherent part of our due process tradition. When that time comes, it is doubtful that the rule of law will be overturned and the foundations of the republic shattered if judicial review is either eliminated entirely or substantially foreshortened. That would be mainly a recognition that there are other vineyards in which the labors of the judicial power, federal and state, are more sorely needed to assure the continuing availability of essential justice.

The New Science of Judicial Administration

The central fact as we face forward is the staggering volume of litigation with which both state and federal courts are being called upon to cope. Whatever may be the lightening of the load in the future through wider employment of the administrative process, the business of the courts will continue to be great and growing. It is providential rather than otherwise that the organization of judicial power in this country has provided so many functioning courts to deal with the challenge. Our present task is to organize the relationships between them in such manner as to realize from them the highest total efficiency. This can hardly imply the complete subordination of the one to the other. It does imply a division of jurisdiction between them along rational lines which assumes the capacity of each to do its job competently.

The setting of the house in order to this end is not just

a matter for the states. The federal courts have much need for critical self-examination; and the place to begin is with the vaunted system of selection and tenure, supposedly the brightest jewel in the federal judicial crown. The greatest need at the moment is that there be brought to bear upon the disposition of controversies the maximum amount of judicial man-hours; and yet thousands of these are being lost annually through inordinate and inexcusable delays in filling vacancies. In my time on my court there have been delays of as much as a year. Our trial court is in desperate straits with a criminal backlog approaching a point where there is real danger that indictments must be dismissed for denial of the constitutional right to a speedy trial—and yet there is a vacancy which has endured for more than a year. I have never believed that the volume of crime is significantly responsive to what the courts do doctrinally, but I have come to think that crime rises as the time increases from initial arrest to final disposition; and delay is currently the greatest weakness in the administration of criminal justice. An American Bar Association committee, going back quite a few years, has annually made a study of the federal judicial time lost through delay in filling vacancies. On the whole, their statistics tell a sorry tale.[38] An appointive system which does not appoint is hardly in a position to look down its nose at an elective one. The friends of the federal approach must search out the causes of its dilatoriness and seek to end them, whether they are found to be in the White House or on Capitol Hill.

There is also the matter of tenure. The constitutional protections afforded federal judges [39] in this regard are assuredly wise; but the values they serve do not require that the incompetent, ailing, or aging judge retain his seat as long as he chooses. Removal of a corrupt judge has been an infinitesimal problem in the long history of the federal bench. What is needed is to substitute a uniform rule of compulsion for the exercise of individual discretion in the matter of retirement, together with incentives for early retirement from active service of the hale and hearty in order that they may, by continuing to sit as senior judges, swell the total judicial resources. There is much that could appear to be done to effect reform within the limits of Article III, but, to the extent that it is found to stand in the way, amendment is imperative. In this area, at any rate, several of the states are leading the way with successful means of getting at the problem, means which the Congress would do well to mark carefully.[40]

There is a ferment of change generally at the state level. Each year sees advances here and there in the matter of selection and tenure. The Missouri Plan is well into its second quarter-century, and its influence is strongly apparent and rising. Nominating commissions and judicial selection boards are making their appearance more widely. Salaries are being increased, and retirement and death benefits improved. A leaf from the federal book is being taken in the matter of continuing judicial education, and this is perhaps one of the most interesting and promising developments of all. Helped greatly by the support and leadership of the Honorable Tom Clark, only lately retired as an active Justice of the United States Supreme Court, the state judges at both the trial and appellate levels are aggressively pursuing new opportunities to broaden their knowledge and understanding of their craft.[41] The National College of State Trial Judges now has its permanent home on the campus of the University of Nevada; California, aided by a Ford Foundation grant, is experimenting with a similar institution at the state level. The Oregon Legislature in 1965 took the ultimately enlightened step of authorizing sabbatical years for self-improving reflection and study for the judges of that state's highest court.[42] This last surely blunts any claim for the federal system of unrelieved superiority!

The state courts have not been backward either in addressing themselves to modernizing the purely administrative framework of judicial proceedings.[43] This is the field in which great changes seem almost certain to occur throughout the next decade. The rising volume of cases taxes the record-keeping and scheduling facilities of the courts, as well as their decisional capabilities. There must be summoned to their aid the newest technology in data processing, information storage and retrieval, and programming of all kinds, including the assembly of jurors, the summoning of parties and witnesses, and the calendaring of hearings. The computer is obviously the court clerk of tomorrow. Moreover, it should work as a mechanical adjunct of a responsible court administrator who approximates the judges in salary and prestige, and who does everything except decide cases. Without such an official at the present time, judges are unduly diverted from their true function to time-consuming administrative tasks, and there is a serious loss in the number of judicial man-hours available for that work which only a judge can do, namely, the hearing and decision of lawsuits.

In the federal system certainly, there is an urgent need for active management of the court's business, over and above the merely passive function of keeping statistics. Every federal circuit should, I believe, have a single administrator who is responsible for the efficient functioning of that circuit, although not, of course, for the law it makes. His authority should extend to the preliminary screening of cases for the purpose of determining how they should be handled; his competence should encompass all aspects of the court's internal functioning and its external relations, except those involving the resolution of cases. It is not farfetched to speculate that a national conference of such officers might do more to expedite the work of the federal courts than the present Judicial Conference of the United States, constituted as the latter now is of active judges heavily burdened with decisional responsibilities. It would, in any event, be an essential adjunct of a new Federal Judicial Center of the kind now being considered by Congress.[44]

A new and expanding science of judicial administration holds out the promise of satisfying and responsible careers in public service for professional men trained in the law, and reputations are to be made which may well overshadow the accomplishments of some of those who wear the black robes. The persistent law school preoccupation with appellate opinions could usefully shift, in some degree, to a concern with the rationality of the course of the proceedings from which those opinions, often at too long last, eventually emerge.

The Longer View

Judicial power has, for better or worse, become a major instrument in the formation of social, economic, and political policy. It has, of course, always been such to some extent, at least for those with the means to invoke it. But, thanks to the extraordinarily enlarging contours of equal protection and due process, it now lies at the hand of vastly greater numbers of our citizens for whom it has largely been heretofore a remote and forbidding abstraction. The mature corporation lawyer serving as court-appointed counsel in a criminal case, and the recent law school graduate working in a neighborhood law office of the poverty program, can give convincing testimony to this effect. And the seeming miracles being wrought in the courts on behalf of the disadvantaged are, in turn, stimulating new and ingenious assertions of legal right and injury by those of a more exalted economic status. Government at all levels finds its policies and actions increasingly challenged from every side by appeals for judicial intervention.

There are searching questions to be asked as to whether this development is wholly healthy, at least to the extent that it reflects cynicism about the responsiveness of legislative or executive policy to the political processes. It may be easier to file a lawsuit than to run for office, but it is not necessarily a better way to run the country. The judicial pendulum swings, and mine is a generation before whom our law professors incessantly paraded the then mischiefs of government by judiciary. These are, however, philosophical issues going to the very nature of our ideals of self-government. They are outside the range of this inquiry except to note that the future effectiveness and integrity of the judicial power depend in no small degree upon the purification of the political processes to a point where there is a renewal of faith in the potency of the elective sanction. Then there may be a greater readiness to heed Justice Stone's famous admonition that "courts are not the only agency of government that must be assumed to have capacity to govern." [45]

The tasks appropriate to the judicial power, however, will at all events be manifold and significant. Their importance demands the best we can muster in terms of the rational organization of that power for their accomplishment. Their nature at the moment and for the foreseeable future would seem to place them among those of our problems calling for a larger measure of decentralized handling. The "one supreme Court" of Article III has a great mission to perform, but it cannot begin to see that justice is done in every lawsuit that is filed throughout the land. Its effectiveness has been critically enhanced by the Congressional determination to provide inferior federal courts. But it also seems clear, as we view the mounting flood of litigation at this point in the life of the nation, that the availability of the state courts to help man the dikes is of providential significance.

If, as appears likely, the compelling problems of our time prefigure a renascence of localized government, then the state courts now stand on the threshold of larger things. To weld them into a harmonious and productive relationship with their federal counterparts is an imperative for all who conceive of the judicial power as an indispensable instrument of civilized government.

NOTES

I. THE PHENOMENON OF DUAL COURT SYSTEMS

1. Washington Post, March 19, 1967, at A–8, col. 3.
2. *Id.* at col. 4.
3. W. Heller, New Dimensions of Political Economy 121 (1966), quoting remarks of Richard C. Goodwin to visiting foreign students, July 20, 1965, p. 4 (White House press release).
4. "It is possible to predict that the first party to carry this banner (if buttressed by a solid program) will find itself on the right side of the decisive issue of the 1970's." Goodwin, *The Shape of American Politics*, Commentary, June 1967, at 25, 36.
5. Brennan, *The Responsibilities of the Legal Profession*, 54 A.B.A.J. 121, 125 (1968).

6. Washington Post, March 19, 1967, at A–8, col. 6.
7. See N. Rockefeller, The Future of Federalism (1962 Godkin Lectures at Harvard University); T. Sanford, Storm Over the States (1967); Stevenson, *Who Runs the Gambling Machines?*, 189 Atlantic Monthly 35 (Feb. 1952).
8. See Reynolds v. Sims, 377 U.S. 533 (1964); Wesberry v. Sanders, 376 U.S. 1 (1964); Gray v. Sanders, 372 U.S. 368 (1963); Baker v. Carr, 369 U.S. 186 (1962); Friedelbaum, *Baker v. Carr: The New Doctrine of Judicial Intervention and its Implications for American Federalism*, 29 U. Chi. L. Rev. 673 (1962); Neal, *Baker v. Carr: Politics in Search of Law*, in The Supreme Court *Review* 252 (P. Kurland ed. 1962); Note, *Reapportionment*, 79 Harv. L. Rev. 1228 (1966). In 1962 Friedelbaum concluded that "[t]he state courts, armed with the fourteenth amendment, can serve as the most effective instrument for attaining long-sought objectives [of reapportionment] with a minimum of direct federal involvement." 29 U. Chi. L. Rev. at 704.
9. See W. Heller, *supra* note 3; Heller and Pechman, *Questions and Answers on Revenue Sharing* (The Brookings Institution, Studies of Government Finance Reprint No. 135, 1967).
10. U.S. Const. art. III, §§ 1–2:

> The judicial Power of the United States, shall be vested in one supreme Court, and in such inferior Courts as the Congress may from time to time ordain and establish.
>
> . . . .
>
> The judicial Power shall extend to all Cases, in Law and Equity, arising under this Constitution,

the Laws of the United States, and Treaties made, or which shall be made, under their authority;—to all Cases affecting Ambassadors, other public Ministers and Consuls;—to all Cases of admiralty and maritime Jurisdiction;—to Controversies to which the United States shall be a Party;—to Controversies between two or more States;—between a State and Citizens of another State;—between Citizens of different States,—between Citizens of the same State claiming Lands under Grants of different States, and between a State, or the Citizens thereof, and foreign States, Citizens or Subjects.

Compare, e.g., Va. Const. art. VI, § 87:

The judicial power of the State shall be vested in a Supreme Court of Appeals, circuit courts, city courts, and such other courts, inferior to the Supreme Court of Appeals, as are hereinafter authorized, or as may be hereafter established by law. The jurisdiction of these tribunals, and of the judges thereof, except so far as conferred by this Constitution, shall be regulated by law.

11. The Federalist No. 78, at 522–23 (J. Cooke ed. 1961) (Hamilton).
12. The Federalist Nos. 22, 78–92 (Hamilton).
13. See, e.g., F. Frankfurter & J. Landis, The Business of the Supreme Court, A Study in the Federal Judicial System (1927); H. M. Hart & H. Wechsler, The Federal Courts and the Federal System (1953); C. Warren, The Making of the Constitution (1937); Frank, *Historical Bases of the Federal Judicial System*, 13 Law & Contemp. Prob. 3 (1948); Frankfurter, *Distribution of Judicial Power Between United States and State Courts*, 13 Cornell L. Q. 499 (1928); Friendly, *The Historic Bases of Diver-*

sity Jurisdiction, 41 Harv. L. Rev. 483 (1928); Warren, *New Light on the History of the Federal Judiciary Act of 1789*, 37 Harv. L. Rev. 49 (1923).

14. See, e.g., P. Freund, On Understanding the Supreme Court (1950); C. Hughes, The Supreme Court of the United States (1928); C. Warren, The Supreme Court in United States History (rev. ed. 1937).

15. Freund, *The Federal Judiciary*, in Studies in Federalism 115–16 (Bowie & Friedrich eds. 1954).

16. Section 101 of the British North America Act, 1867, 30 & 31 Vict., c,3, provides that the Canadian Parliament may

> provide for the Constitution, Maintenance, and Organization of a General Court of Appeals for Canada, and for the Establishment of any additional Courts for the Better Administration of the Laws of Canada.

17. Walz, *Canada, In Her Centennial Year, Weighs the Future*, New York Times, Jan. 2, 1967, at 2, col. 2.

18. Brown v. Board of Educ., 347 U.S. 483 (1954). See Bickel, *The Original Understanding and the Segregation Decision*, 69 Harv. L. Rev. 1 (1955); Black, *The Lawfulness of the Segregation Decisions*, 69 Yale L. J. 421 (1960); Fairman, *The Attack on the Segregation Cases*, 70 Harv. L. Rev. 83 (1956).

19. Brown v. Board of Educ. 349 U.S. 294 (1955). On the problems of enforcement, see, e.g., McKay, *"With All Deliberate Speed": Legislative Reaction and Judicial Development 1956–1957*, 43 Va. L. Rev. 1205 (1957).

20. See, e.g., Banzhaf, *Multi-Member Electoral Districts— Do They Violate the "One Man, One Vote" Principle*, 75 Yale L. J. 1309 (1966); Banzhaf, *Weighted Voting*

Doesn't Work: A Mathematical Analysis, 19 Rutgers L. Rev. 317 (1965); Nagel, *Simplified Bipartisan Computer Redistricting*, 17 Stan. L. Rev. 863 (1965); Weaver & Hess, *A Procedure for Nonpartisan Districting: Development of Computer Techniques*, 73 Yale L. J. 288 (1963).

21. See, e.g., United States v. Wade, 388 U.S. 218 (1967); Berger v. New York, 388 U.S. 41 (1967); Miranda v. Arizona, 387 U.S. 436 (1966).

22. See, e.g., Gojack v. United States, 384 U.S. 702 (1966); Barenblatt v. United States, 360 U.S. 109 (1959); Watkins v. United States, 354 U.S. 178 (1957); Sweezy v. New Hampshire, 354 U.S. 234 (1957).

23. See, e.g., Kent v. Dulles, 357 U.S. 116 (1958); Lynd v. Rusk, 128 U.S. App. D.C. 399, 389 F.2d 940 (1967); cf. Youngstown Sheet & Tube Co. v. Sawyer, 343 U.S. 579 (1952).

24. Cf. Powell v. McCormack, 395 F.2d 577 (D.C. Cir., 1968) *Petition for cert. pending*, no. 138, 1968 term.

25. Federalisms whose federal judiciary is limited to a single high court include Germany and Switzerland. See R. Bowie & C. Friedrich, Studies in Federalism 140–65 (1954). Australia, like Canada (see note 16 *supra* and accompanying text), has never exercised its constitutional discretion to create lower federal courts:

> The judicial power of the Commonwealth shall be vested in a Federal Supreme Court, to be called the High Court of Australia, and in such other federal courts as the Parliament creates, and in such other courts as it invests with federal jurisdiction.

Commonwealth of Australia Constitution Act of 1900, § 71, 63 & 64 Vict., c.12. For a general discussion of foreign judiciary systems, see Riesenfeld & Hazard, *Fed-*

eral Courts in Foreign Systems, 13 Law & Contemp. Prob. 29 (1948).

26. For accounts of the circumstances of the drafting of the Constitution and the first Judiciary acts, see authorities cited in note 13 *supra.*

27. Using the fiscal 1968 Budget figures of $96 million for the federal judiciary as compared with a total budget of $186.5 billion, the ratio is approximately 1:1950.

28. Quoted in C. Warren, The Making of the Constitution at 326 (1937).

29. *Id.*

30. *Id.* at 327.

31. 1 Stat. 73 (1789).

32. Quoted in Warren, *New Light on the History of the Federal Judiciary Act of 1789,* 37 Harv. L. Rev. 49, 66 (1923).

33. Id.

34. *Id.,* Letter from Edward Carrington to James Monroe, Sept. 15, 1788.

35. The Federalist No. 81, at 547 (J. Cooke ed. 1961) (Hamilton).

36. Warren, *supra* note 32, at 53.

37. *Id.* at 60–61, letter from Ellsworth to Judge Richard Law of Connecticut, April 30, 1789.

38. Letter from Ames to George Minot, Sept. 3, 1789, in I Works of Fisher Ames 69 (S. Ames ed. 1854).

39. See Martin v. Hunter's Lessee, 14 U.S. (1 Wheat.) 304, 327–30 (1816); see also Warren, *supra* note 32, at 68.

40. Letter from Edward Carrington of Virginia to Madison, Aug. 3, 1789, in Warren, *supra* note 32, at 110.

41. Samuel Livermore of New Hampshire, quoted in Warren, *supra* note 32, at 123.

42. William Smith of South Carolina, in Warren, *supra* note 32, at 123.

43. Quoted in Warren, *supra* note 32, at 124.
44. Quoted in F. Frankfurter & J. Landis, *supra* note 13, at 8 n.
45. The true motivation for the federal diversity jurisdiction remains in some doubt. The conventional historical explanation is that given by Warren in 1923:

> The chief and only real reason for this diverse citizenship jurisdiction was to afford a tribunal in which a foreigner or citizen of another State might have the law administered free from the local prejudices or passions which might prevail in a State Court against foreigners or non-citizens.

Warren, *supra* note 32, at 83. This assumption was challenged in 1928 by Judge Friendly. He argued that there is no evidence that local prejudice prevailed in 1789, and that the framers and Congress were more interested in other things:

> The real fear was not so much of state courts as of state legislatures. . . . the desire to protect creditors against legislation favorable to debtors was a principal reason for the grant of diversity jurisdiction, and . . . as a reason it was by no means without validity.

Friendly, *supra* note 13, at 495–97. Compare Yntema & Jaffin, *Preliminary Analysis of Concurrent Jurisdiction*, 79 U. Pa. L. Rev. 869 (1931). Frank has taken an intermediate view, concluding that diversity jurisdiction was the product of several factors:

1. The desire to avoid regional prejudice against commercial litigants. . . .
2. The desire to permit commercial . . . interests to litigate their controversies . . . before judges

who would be firmly tied to their own interests.
3. The desire to achieve more efficient administration of justice for the classes thus benefitted.

Frank, *supra* note 13, at 28. For further discussion of the sources and merits of diversity jurisdiction, see H. M. Hart & H. Wechsler, *supra* note 13, at 891–97, and authorities cited therein.

46. Articles criticizing the diversity jurisdiction include Field, *Diversity of Jurisdiction: A Response to Judge Wright*, 13 Wayne L. Rev. 489 (1967); Field, *Proposals on Federal Diversity Jurisdiction*, 17 So. Carolina L. Rev. 669 (1965); Frankfurter, *supra* note 13; Friendly, *supra* note 13.

47. See, e.g., Frank, *For Maintaining Diversity Jurisdiction*, 73 Yale L. J. 7 (1963); Moore & Weckstein, *Diversity Jurisdiction: Past, Present and Future*, 43 Tex. L. Rev. 1 (1964), J. S. Wright, *The Federal Courts and the Nature and Quality of State Law*, 13 Wayne L. Rev. 317 (1967).

48. Act of Feb. 13, 1801, § 11, 2 Stat. 89, 92. This statute was repealed by the Act of March 8, 1802, 2 Stat. 132.

49. See F. Frankfurter & J. Landis, *supra* note 13, at 64–65.

50. 18 Stat. 470 (1875).

51. F. Frankfurter & J. Landis, *supra* note 13, at 64.

52. One striking example of wholesale replacement of caselaw by statute is the Uniform Commercial Code.

II. THE STRESSES OF COEXISTENCE

1. Texas v. White, 74 U.S. (7 Wall.) 700, 725 (1868).
2. For various views on the Court of the Union proposal, see Symposium, 39 Notre Dame Law. 623 (1964).
3. U.S. Const. art. VI:

This Constitution, and the laws of the United States which shall be made in Pursuance thereof; and all Treaties made, or which shall be made, under the Authority of the United States, shall be the supreme Law of the Land; and the Judges in every State shall be bound thereby, any Thing in the Constitution or Laws of any State to the Contrary notwithstanding.

4. C. Black, Jr., The People and the Court 121 (1960).
5. Brennan, Address to Conference of Chief Justices, August 7, 1964, *Some Aspects of Federalism,* 39 N.Y.U.L. Rev. 945, 946 (1964).
6. See United States v. Coolidge, 14 U.S. (1 Wheat.) 415 (1816); United States v. Hudson and Goodwin, 11 U.S. (7 Cranch) 32 (1812).
7. "There were 30,534 criminal cases filed in the United States district courts during [fiscal] 1967, an increase of almost 3 percent over . . . 1966. . . ." 1967 Ann. Rep. of the Director of the Administrative Office of the United States Courts II–27.
8. 41 U.S. (16 Pet.) 1 (1842).
9. See Warren, *New Light on the History of the Federal Judiciary Act of 1789,* 37 Harv. L. Rev. 49 (1923). See also Friendly, *The Historic Bases of Diversity Jurisdiction,* 41 Harv. L. Rev. 483 (1928); Frankfurter, *Distribution of Judicial Power Between United States and State Courts,* 13 Cornell L. Q. 499 (1928).
10. 304 U.S. 64 (1938).
11. 326 U.S. 99 (1945).
12. 356 U.S. 525 (1958). Critical analyses of Erie's progeny include Quigley, *Congressional Repairs of the Erie Derailment,* 60 Mich. L. Rev. 1031 (1962); Note, *Of Lawyers and Laymen: A Study of Federalism, The Judicial Process and Erie,* 71 Yale L. J. 344 (1961).

13. See, e.g., Clearfield Trust Co. v. United States, 318 U.S. 363 (1943).

14. Friendly, *In Praise of Erie—And of the New Federal Common Law*, 39 N.Y.U.L. Rev. 383 (1964).

15. *Id.* at 407.

16. 1A Moore's Federal Practice ¶ O. 318, n.a (Kurland & Lucas, Supp. 1967). For other commentary on the "new federal common law" see Hill, *The Law-Making Power of the Federal Courts: Constitutional Preemption*, 67 Colum. L. Rev. 1024 (1967); Note, *Exceptions to Erie v. Tompkins: The Survival of Federal Common Law*, 59 Harv. L. Rev. 966 (1946); Note, *Rules of Decision in Nondiversity Suits*, 69 Yale L. J. 1428 (1960).

17. Wallis v. Pan American Petroleum Corp., 384 U.S. 63, 68 (1966).

18. See, e.g., D'Oench, Duhme & Co. v. FDIC, 315 U.S. 447 (1942); Deitrick v. Greaney, 309 U.S. 190 (1940); Postal Telegraph-Cable Co. v. Warren-Godwin Lumber Co., 251 U.S. 27 (1919).

19. See, e.g., United States v. County of Allegheny, 322 U.S. 174 (1944).

20. See, e.g., Priebe & Sons v. United States, 322 U.S. 407 (1947); Federal Crop Ins. Corp. v. Merrill, 332 U.S. 380 (1947); National Metropolitan Bank v. United States, 323 U.S. 454 (1945); Clearfield Trust Co. v. United States, 318 U.S. 363 (1943).

21. See, e.g., Commissioner v. Estate of Bosch, 387 U.S. 456 (1967); United States v. Bess, 357 U.S. 51 (1958); Morgan v. Commissioner, 309 U.S. 78 (1940). See generally Stephens & Freeland, *What Law Controls in Federal Tax Controversies: State or Federal?*, 17 J. Taxation 182 (1962).

22. See Banco National de Cuba v. Sabbatino, 376 U.S. 398 (1964).

23. See, e.g., Bank of America Nat'l Trust & Savings Ass'n v. Parnell, 352 U.S. 29 (1956).
24. Wallis v. Pan American Petroleum Corp., 384 U.S. 63, 68 (1966).
25. *Id.*
26. See generally Cox, *The Supreme Court and the Federal System,* 50 Calif. L. Rev. 800 (1962).
27. Pennsylvania v. Nelson, 350 U.S. 497 (1956).
28. Commonwealth v. Nelson, 377 Pa. 58, 104 A.2d 133 (1954).
29. Uphaus v. Wyman, 360 U.S. 72 (1959). Illustrative of critical comment on the Supreme Court's subversion-pre-emption decisions are Cramton, *Pennsylvania v. Nelson: A Case Study in Federal Pre-emption,* 26 U. Chi. L. Rev. 85 (1958); Note, *Federal Preemption of State Sedition Laws,* 33 So. Cal. L. Rev. 92 (1959).
30. 359 U.S. 236 (1959).
31. Textile Workers Union of America v. Lincoln Mills, 353 U.S. 448 (1957). See Cox, *Federalism in the Law of Labor Relations,* 67 Harv. L. Rev. 1297 (1954); Note, *Section 301 (a) and the Federal Common Law of Labor Agreements,* 75 Yale L. J. 877 (1966); 40 Notre Dame Law. 112 (1964).
32. See Friendly, *supra* note 14, at 413–14.
33. U.S. Const. amend. 14, § 1:

> No State shall make or enforce any law which shall abridge the privileges or immunities of citizens of the United States; nor shall any State deprive any person of life, liberty, or property, without due process of law; nor deny to any person within its jurisdiction the equal protection of the laws.

A perceptive assessment of the clash is found in Allen, *The Supreme Court, Federalism, and State Systems of Criminal Justice,* 8 De Paul L. Rev. 213 (1959).

34. U.S. Const. art. I, § 9:

> The Privilege of the Writ of Habeas Corpus shall not be suspended, unless when in Cases of Rebellion or Invasion the public Safety may require it.

For background on the history and nature of the writ, see Oaks, *Habeas Corpus in the States—1776–1865*, 32 U. Chi. L. Rev. 243 (1965).

35. Schaefer, Oliver Wendell Holmes Lecture at the Harvard Law School, April 1955, *Federalism and State Criminal Procedure*, 70 Harv. L. Rev. 1, 26 (1956).

36. 28 U.S.C. § 2254 (Supp. II, 1965–66).

37. 344 U.S. 443 (1953).

38. H. R. 5649, 84th Cong., 1st Sess. (1955).

39. Letter from Henry P. Chandler, Director of the Administrative Office of the United States Courts, to Hon. Sam Rayburn, Speaker of the House of Representatives, April 11, 1955, in *Hearings on H. R. 5649 Before Subcomm. No. 3 of the House Comm. on the Judiciary*, 84th Cong., 1st Sess. 2 (1955).

40. *Hearings, supra* note 39, at 3.

41. *Id.* at 6.

42. Before 1948 a similar abuse was encountered from those in federal custody—"the review of a proceeding in a Federal court by another Federal court of coordinate jurisdiction." *Hearings, supra* note 39, at 3. In 1948 this situation was remedied by the enactment of 28 U.S.C. § 2255 (1964), which requires federal prisoners who seek to attack their convictions collaterally to "move the court which imposed the sentence to vacate, set aside or correct the sentence." Furthermore, under Section 2255, "the sentencing court shall not be required to entertain a second or successive motion for similar relief on behalf of the same prisoner."

43. 372 U.S. 391 (1963).
44. 372 U.S. 293 (1963).
45. In fiscal year 1967, 7,246 habeas corpus petitions—and a total of 10,243 prisoners' petitions—were filed in the United States District Courts. 1967 Ann. Rep. of the Director of the Administrative Office of the United States Courts II–20, Table C–2.
46. Some of the voices are Bator, *Finality in Criminal Law and Federal Habeas Corpus for State Prisoners*, 76 Harv. L. Rev. 441 (1963); Carter, *The Use of Federal Habeas Corpus By State Prisoners*, 23 Wash. & Lee L. Rev. 23 (1966); Desmond, *Federal and State Habeas Corpus: How to Make Two Parallel Judicial Lines Meet*, 49 A.B.A.J. 1166 (1963); Note, *State Court Withdrawal from Habeas Corpus*, 114 U. Pa. L. Rev. 1081 (1966). Compare Justice Brennan's William H. Leary Lecture to the Utah Law School, October 26, 1961, *Federal Habeas Corpus and State Prisoners: An Exercise in Federalism*, 7 Utah L. Rev. 423 (1961); Wright & Sofaer, *Federal Habeas Corpus for State Prisoners: The Allocation of Fact-Finding Responsibility*, 75 Yale L. J. 895 (1966).
47. A thorough discussion of the subject of anti-suit injunctions is Comment, *Anti-Suit Injunctions Between State and Federal Courts*, 32 U. Chi. L. Rev. 471 (1965).
48. Act of March 2, 1793, ch. 22, § 5, 1 Stat. 335.
49. See generally Durfee & Sloss, *Federal Injunction Against Proceedings in State Courts: The Life History of a Statute*, 30 Mich. L. Rev. 1145 (1932); Note, *Federal Power to Enjoin State Court Proceedings*, 74 Harv. L. Rev. (1961).
50. 314 U.S. 118 (1941).
51. 28 U.S.C. § 2283 (1964).
52. H. R. Rep. No. 308, 80th Cong., 1st Sess. A 181 (1948).

53. Comment, *supra* note 48, at 482.
54. Amalgamated Clothing Workers of America v. Richman Bros. Co., 348 U.S. 511, 518 (1955).
55. 380 U.S. 479 (1965).
56. ALI Study of the Division of Jurisdiction Between State and Federal Courts 176, Commentary § 1372 (Tent. Draft No. 5, 1967).
57. § 1372 (Tent. Draft No. 5, 1967).
58. The draft provision was approved by the membership at the 1967 Annual Meeting on May 16, 1967. 1967 ALI Proceedings 172, 174.
59. See Arnold, *State Power to Enjoin Federal Court Proceedings*, 51 Va. L. Rev. 59 (1965); Comment, *supra* note 48, at 497–98.
60. 377 U.S. 408 (1964).
61. Arnold, *supra* note 60, at 75.
62. *See* § 1373 and Note (Tent. Draft No. 5, 1967).
63. ALI Study, *supra* note 57, at 189, Commentary § 1373 (Tent. Draft No. 5, 1967), quoting in part from Comment, *supra* note 48, at 472.
64. U.S. Const. amend. XI:

> The Judicial power of the United States shall not be construed to extend to any suit in law or equity, commenced or prosecuted against one of the United States by Citizens of another State, or by Citizens or Subjects of any Foreign State.

65. *Ex Parte* Young, 209 U.S. 123 (1908).
66. See Lockwood, Maw, & Rosenberry, *The Use of the Federal Injunction in Constitutional Litigation*, 43 Harv. L. Rev. 425 (1930).
67. Act of June 18, 1910, 36 Stat. 557, as amended, 28 U.S.C. § 2281 (1964). See generally Currie, *The Three-Judge District Court in Constitutional Litigation*, 32 U. Chi. L. Rev. 1 (1964).

68. Tax Injunction Act of 1937, 50 Stat. 738, as amended, 28 U.S.C. § 1341 (1964).
69. Johnson Act of 1934, 48 Stat. 775, as amended, 28 U.S.C. § 1342 (1964).
70. See generally C. Wright, *The Abstention Doctrine Revisited*, 37 Texas L. Rev. 815 (1959); Note, *Federal-Question Abstention: Justice Frankfurter's Doctrine in an Activist Era*, 80 Harv. L. Rev. 604 (1967); Note, *Abstention and Certification in Diversity Suits: "Perfection of Means and Confusion of Goals,"* 73 Yale L. J. 850 (1964).
71. 312 U.S. 496 (1941).
72. Spector Motor Service, Inc. v. McLaughlin, 323 U.S. 101 (1941), ordering abstention, was finally disposed of in Spector Motor Service, Inc. v. O'Connor, 340 U.S. 602 (1951). Louisiana Power & Light Co. v. City of Thibodaux, 360 U.S. 25 (1959) ordered abstention in a case which had been commenced in February 1957; the litigation was finally terminated in December 1963 by City of Thibodaux v. Louisiana Power & Light Co., 225 F. Supp. 657 (E.D. La. 1963).
73. See, e.g., NAACP v. Button, 371 U.S. 415 (1963), disposing of the litigation after the Supreme Court had ordered abstention in Harrison v. NAACP, 360 U.S. 167 (1959).
74. Zwickler v. Koota, 389 U.S. 241 (1967); Harman v. Forssenius, 380 U.S. 528 (1965); Dombrowski v. Pfister, 380 U.S. 479 (1965); Davis v. Mann, 377 U.S. 678 (1964); Baggett v. Bullitt, 377 U.S. 360 (1964); Hostetter v. Idlewild Bon Voyage Liquor Corp., 377 U.S. 324 (1964); Griffin v. County School Bd., 377 U.S. 218 (1964); McNeese v. Board of Educ., 373 U.S. 668 (1963).
75. Baggett v. Bullitt, 377 U.S. 360, 378–79 (1964).

76. See 1966 Handbook of the National Conference of Commissioners on Uniform State Laws 94–95.

77. Fla. Stat. § 25.031 (1967); Hawaii Rev. Laws §§ 214–26, 27, as amended by Hawaii Laws 1965, Act 8; Me. Rev. Stat. Ann., tit. 4, § 57 (Supp. 1967); Wash. Rev. Code Ann., c. 2.60 (Supp. 1967).

78. § 1371 (d) (Tent. Draft No. 5, 1967).

79. Note, *Federal Question Abstention: Justice Frankfurter's Doctrine in an Activist Era*, 80 Harv. L. Rev. 604, 620 (1967).

80. § 1371 (c) (e) (Tent. Draft No. 5, 1967).

81. Letter from Jefferson to Spencer Roane, June 27, 1821, quoted in Mason, *The Supreme Court and Federalism*, 44 Texas L. Rev. 1187, 1208 (1966).

III. THE QUEST FOR ACCOMMODATION

1. Johnson, *What Adlai Stevenson Left Us*, book review, The New Republic, Nov. 11, 1967, at 21.

2. The chronic alcoholic may be on his way out of the criminal law. See Easter v. District of Columbia, 124 U.S. App. D.C. 33, 361 F.2d 50 (1966); Driver v. Hinnant, 356 F.2d 761 (4th Cir. 1966); but see Powell v. Texas, 392 U.S. 514 (1968). England's recent relaxation of the criminal law relating to homosexuality is perhaps a straw in the wind. See generally Dworkin, *Lord Devlin and the Enforcement of Morals*, 75 Yale L. J. 986 (1966).

3. New York Times Co. v. Sullivan, 376 U.S. 254 (1964).

4. See Rosenblatt v. Baer, 383 U.S. 75 (1966); and see The Washington Post Co. v. Keogh, 125 U.S. App. D.C. 43, 365 F.2d 965 (1966), *cert. denied*, 385 U.S. 1011 (1967).

5. See generally The Courts, the Public, and the Law Explosion (H. Jones ed. 1965).

6. See Commissioner v. Tellier, 383 U.S. 687 (1966), allowing deduction—as an ordinary and necessary business expense under Int. Rev. Code of 1954, § 162—of legal fees incurred in the unsuccessful defense of a criminal prosecution. See generally Brookes, *Litigation Expenses and the Income Tax,* 14 Tax L. Rev. 241 (1957).

7. During its 1966 Term, the Supreme Court acted on 2503 petitions for certiorari. See *The Supreme Court, 1966 Term,* 81 Harv. L. Rev. 69, 127 (1967).

8. 1967 Ann. Rep. of the Director of the Administrative Office of the United States Courts I–4, I–6.

9. In fiscal 1968 $38 million of Congressionally appropriated monies were available for the OEO's Legal Services Program, and the fiscal 1969 budget request is $42 million.

10. New York Times, Oct. 8, 1967, § 1, at 70, cols. 4–5.

11. See, e.g., Smith v. King, 277 F. Supp. 31 (M. D. Ala. 1967) (striking down Alabama's "substitute father" rule); Krebs v. Ashbrook, 275 F. Supp. 111 (D.D.C. 1967); Thompson v. Shapiro, 270 F. Supp. 331 (D. Conn. 1967), *prob. juris. noted,* 389 U.S. 1032 (1968) (both striking down state residency requirements). Cf. Fox v. Michigan Employment Security Comm'n, 379 Mich. 579, 153 N.W. 2d 644 (1967). See generally Reich, *Individual Rights and Social Welfare: The Emerging Legal Issues,* 74 Yale L. J. 1245 (1965); Note, *Federal Judicial Review of State Welfare Practices,* 67 Colum. L. Rev. 84 (1967).

12. Dunmar v. Ailes, 121 U.S. App. D.C. 45, 348 F.2d 51 (1965).

13. Luftig v. McNamara, 252 F. Supp. 819 (D.D.C. 1966), *aff'd per curiam,* 126 U.S. App. D.C. 4, 373 F.2d 664, *cert. denied sub nom.* Mora v. McNamara, 389 U.S. 934

(1967). The Selective Service System also is increasingly being called into court. See Wolff v. Selective Serv. Local Bd. No. 16, 372 F.2d 817 (2d Cir. 1967); Layton & Fine, *The Draft and Exhaustion of Administrative Remedies*, 56 Geo. L. J. 315 (1967).

14. Protestants and Other Americans United for Separation of Church and State v. O'Brien, 272 F. Supp. 712 (D.D.C. 1967).

15. Cf. Talley v. Stephens, 247 F. Supp. 683 (E.D. Ark. 1965); Fulwood v. Clemmer, 206 F. Supp. 370 (D.D.C. 1962).

16. E.g., Rouse v. Cameron, 125 U.S. App. D.C. 366, 373 F. 2d 451 (1966).

17. Avins v. Rutgers, 385 F.2d 151 (3d Cir. 1967), *cert. denied*, 390 U.S. 920 (1968).

18. See, e.g., Anderson, *The Line Between Federal and State Court Jurisdiction*, 63 Mich. L. Rev. 1203 (1965).

19. 1959 ALI Proceedings 33.

20. §§ 1301–07 (Official Draft No. 1, 1965).

21. §§ 1311–15 (Tent. Draft No. 5, 1967).

22. See ALI Study of the Division of Jurisdiction Between State and Federal Courts 47–56, Commentary, General Statement (Official Draft No. 1, 1965).

23. See ALI Study of the Division of Jurisdiction Between State and Federal Courts 57–65, Commentary, General Statement (Tent. Draft No. 5, 1967).

24. The draft was approved by the membership at the 1965 Annual Meeting on May 18, 1965. 1965 ALI Proceedings 98–99. The principal thrust of the ALI proposal is that "no person can invoke [diversity] jurisdiction, either originally or on removal, in any district in a State of which he is a citizen." § 1302 (a) (Official Draft No. 1, 1965).

25. Opponents of the diversity proposals include Frank, *For*

Maintaining Diversity Jurisdiction, 73 Yale L. J. 7 (1963); Frank, *Federal Diversity Jurisdiction—An Opposing View*, 17 So. Carolina L. Rev. 677 (1965); Moore & Weckstein, *Diversity Jurisdiction: Past, Present, and Future*, 43 Texas L. Rev. 1 (1964); J. S. Wright, *The Federal Courts and the Nature and Quality of State Law*, 13 Wayne L. Rev. 317 (1967). Professor Field, Reporter to the ALI's Study, has led the defense of the Institute's draft. See Field, *Diversity of Citizenship: A Response to Judge Wright*, 13 Wayne L. Rev. 489 (1967); Field, *Proposals on Federal Diversity Jurisdiction*, 17 So. Carolina L. Rev. 669 (1965).

26. See, e.g., A. Ehrenzweig, "Full Aid" Insurance for the Traffic Victim (1954); L. Green, Traffic Victims: Tort Law and Insurance (1958); Blum & Kalven, *Public Law Perspectives on a Private Law Problem—Auto Compensation Plans*, 31 U. Chi. L. Rev. 641 (1964); Conard, *The Economic Treatment of Automobile Injuries*, 63 Mich. L. Rev. 279 (1964); James, *The Columbia Study of Compensation for Automobile Accidents; An Unanswered Challenge*, 59 Colum. L. Rev. 408 (1959); Keeton & O'Connell, *Basic Protection—A Proposal for Improving Automobile Claims Systems*, 78 Harv. L. Rev. 329 (1964); Morris & Paul, *The Financial Impact of Automobile Accidents*, 110 U. Pa. L. Rev. 913 (1962).

27. On August 15, 1967 the Massachusetts House of Representatives passed with a wide majority a version of the Keeton-O'Connell Basic Protection plan, but it was defeated in the Senate, 28 to 10, on September 18, 1967. See Brainard, *The Rise and Fall of Basic Protection in Massachusetts*, 1967 Ins. L. J. 724 (Dec. 1967).

28. See, e.g., Brennan, *Remarks on Discovery*, in *Symposium—Discovery in Federal Criminal Cases*, 33 F.R.D.

47, 56 (1963); Goldstein, *The State and the Accused: Balance of Advantage in Criminal Procedure*, 69 Yale L. J. 1149, 1172–99 (1960); Traynor, *Ground Lost and Found in Criminal Discovery*, 39 N.Y.U.L. Rev. 228 (1964); *Developments in the Law—Discovery*, 74 Harv. L. Rev. 940, 1051–63 (1961).

29. Less than unanimous verdicts in criminal cases were authorized by the Criminal Justice Act of 1967, c. 80, § 13. South Australia and Tasmania have also abandoned the rule of unanimity. See Address by Lord Denning to the Fourteenth Legal Convention of the Law Council of Australia, July 12, 1967, 41 Aust. L. J. 224, 225–26 (1967). On the decline of the role of the civil jury in England, see R. Jackson, The Machinery of Justice in England 66–68 (4th ed. 1964).

30. See Hazard, *After the Trial—the Realities of Appellate Review*, in The Courts, the Public, and the Law Explosion 60, 82–84 (H. Jones ed. 1965).

31. See C. Wright, *Federal Question Jurisdiction*, 17 So. Carolina L. Rev. 660 (1965); note 23 *supra*.

32. For a state-by-state analysis, see C. Wright, *Procedural Reform in the States*, 24 F.R.D. 85 (1959).

33. See, e.g., Clay, *May the Federal Civil Rules Be Successfully Adopted to Improve State Procedure?: The Kentucky Experience*, 24 F.R.D. 437 (1959); Edenfield, *Significant Features of Federal and Georgia Trial Court Practice and Procedure—A Study and Comparison*, 1 Ga. State Bar J. 315 (1965); Hier, *A "Manifest" Difference Between State and Federal Courts?*, 11 La. B. J. 9 (1963).

34. For discussions and explications of such schemes, see Klein, *Some Basic Problems of Negative Income Taxation*, 1966 Wis. L. Rev. 776; Tobin, Pechman, & Miesz-

kowski, *Is a Negative Income Tax Practical?*, 77 Yale L. J. 1 (1967).

35. See Goldberg, *Interposition—Wild West Water Style*, 17 Stan. L. Rev. 1 (1964). On the problem generally, see Sho Sato, *Water Resources—Comments Upon the Federal-State Relationship*, 48 Calif. L. Rev. 43 (1960).

36. See Trelease, *Water Rights of Various Levels of Government—States' Rights vs. National Powers*, 19 Wyo. L. Rev. 189 (1960). On federal-state compacts generally, see Grad, *Federal-State Compact: A New Experiment in Co-operative Federalism*, 63 Colum. L. Rev. 825 (1963).

37. See Forer, *Water Supply: Suggested Federal Regulation*, 75 Harv. L. Rev. 332 (1961).

38. See, e.g., Report of the Standing Committee on Federal Judiciary, 91 ABA Reports 154, 159 (1966): The 25 existing vacancies "is an alarmingly substantial number. . . . [T]he existing vacancies . . . have remained open much too long."

39. U.S. Const. art. III, § 1:

> The Judges, both of the supreme and inferior Courts, shall hold their Offices during good Behaviour, and shall, at stated Times, receive for their Services, a Compensation, which shall not be diminished during their Continuance in Office.

40. See Winters & Allard, *Judicial Selection and Tenure in the United States*, in The Courts, the Public, and the Law Explosion 146, 166–67 (H. Jones ed. 1965).

41. For an analysis of the work of the Joint Committee for Effective Justice, chaired by Mr. Justice Clark, see Murphee, *Our State Courts—Developments in Judicial Administration*, 37 Miss. L. J. 526 (1966).

42. Ore. Rev. Stat. § 1.290 (1967) permits the Oregon Supreme Court to grant a judge a year's leave without pay if "the administration of justice in Oregon will be enhanced. . . ."

43. See generally Klein & Harris, *Judicial Administration— 1966*, 1966 Annual Survey of American Law 731, 744–51.

44. The Federal Judicial Center was established by Congress in December, 1967. P.L. 90–219, 81 Stat. 664, 28 U.S.C. §§ 620–29. The Center's functions are "to conduct research in all phases of federal judicial administration and to carry on programs of education for federal court connected employees from the judges down." Klein & Harris, *supra* note 43, at 754, n. 146. In signing the bill, President Johnson predicted the Center will "make our federal court system a model for all the courts in all the states and all the cities of America." 13 Amer. Bar News 4 (Jan. 1968).

45. United States v. Butler, 297 U.S. 1, 87 (1936) (dissenting opinion).

PUBLISHED ROSENTHAL
LECTURES 1948–1969

1948 Hazard, John N. "The Soviet Union and International Law," *Illinois Law Review*, XLIII, 591.

1949 Freund, Paul A. *On Understanding the Supreme Court*. Boston: Little, Brown & Co.

1951 Dawson, John P. *Unjust Enrichment, A Comparative Analysis*. Boston: Little, Brown & Co.

1952 Feller, Abraham H. *United Nations and World Community*. Boston: Little, Brown & Co.

1952 Horsky, Charles A. *The Washington Lawyer*. Boston: Little, Brown & Co.

1953 Vanderbilt, Arthur T. "The Essentials of A Sound Judicial System," *Northwestern University Law Review*, XLVIII.

1954 Berle, Adolf A., Jr. *The Twentieth Century Capitalist Revolution*. New York: Harcourt, Brace.

1956 Hurst, James W. *Law and the Conditions of Freedom in the Nineteenth Century United States*. Madison: University of Wisconsin Press.

1956   Sohn, Louis B. "United Nations Charter Revision and the Rule of Law: A Program for Peace," *Northwestern University Law Review*, L, 709.

1956   Gross, Ernest A. "Major Problems in Disarmament," *Northwestern University Law Review*, LI, 299.

1956   Parker, John J. "Dual Sovereignty and the Federal Courts," *Northwestern University Law Review*, LI, 407.

1957   Ukai, Nobushige. "The Individual and the Rule of Law Under the New Japanese Constitution," *Northwestern University Law Review*, LI, 733.

1957   Papale, Antonia Edward. "Judicial Enforcement of Desegregation: Its Problems and Limitations," *Northwestern University Law Review*, LII, 301.

1957   Hart, Herbert L.A. "Murder and the Principles of Punishment: England and the United States," *Northwestern University Law Review*, LII, 433.

1958   Green, Leon. *Traffic Victims: Tort Law and Insurance.* Evanston, Ill.: Northwestern University Press.

1960   Radcliffe, Cyril John. *The Law and Its Compass.* Evanston, Ill.: Northwestern University Press.

1961   Eisenstein, Louis. *The Ideologies of Taxation.* New York: Ronald Press.

1961   Havighurst, Harold C. *The Nature of Private Contract.* Evanston, Ill.: Northwestern University Press.

1962   Pike, James Albert. *Beyond the Law:* the religious and ethical meaning of the lawyer's vocation. New York: Doubleday and Co.

1964   Katz, Wilber G. *Religion and American Constitutions.* Evanston, Ill.: Northwestern University Press.

1965   Cowen, Zelman. *The British Commonwealth of Nations in a Changing World:* law, politics, and prospects. Evanston, Ill.: Northwestern University Press.

1967   Schaefer, Walter V. *The Suspect and Society:* criminal procedure and converging constitutional doctrines. Evanston, Ill.: Northwestern University Press.

1967   Freedman, Max, Beaney, William M., and Rostow, Eugene V. *Perspectives on the Court.* Evanston, Ill.: Northwestern University Press.

1968   Donner, André M. *The Role of the Lawyer in the European Communities.* Evanston, Ill.: Northwestern University Press.

1969   McGowan, Carl. *The Organization of Judicial Power in the United States.* Evanston, Ill.: Northwestern University Press.

A NOTE ON MANUFACTURE

THE TEXT OF THIS BOOK was set on the Linotype in a face called JANSON, an "Old Face" of the Dutch school cut in Amsterdam by the Hungarian, Nickolas Kis, *circa* 1690. *Janson*'s authorship was long attributed erroneously to Anton Janson, a Hollander who had been employed in Leipzig where the matrices were re-discovered. These same mats are today in the possession of the Stempel foundry, Frankfurt, and the machine-cast version you are reading was modelled directly on type produced from the original strikes.

The book was composed, printed, and bound by KINGSPORT PRESS, INC., Kingsport, Tennessee. WARREN PAPER COMPANY manufactured the paper. The typography and binding designs are by *Guy Fleming*.